WHAT'S
FOR
DINNER?

With very best wishes!

This book is dedicated to each and
every one of our foodie customers.

It is most humbling to be part of your lives, to be
trusted with feeding your families and to hear so
much of your feedback. We all get a kick out of
hearing about how your children are learning
how to cook, or that your other half is now your
household's head chef. We also take great delight
in being told that you've learnt a new cooking
technique or tried a vegetable you've never
enjoyed up until now.

It's your feedback that makes us strive to do better
— we read all of your comments and thank you
for your honesty, your humour and your belief in
us. You've helped us learn and you've continued
to give us so much support. We love you guys —
you all rock!

Thanks!

WHAT'S FOR DINNER?

80 WEEKNIGHT FAVOURITES

**MY FOOD BAG
& NADIA LIM**

A&U

CONTENTS

THIS BOOK IS CRAMMED FULL OF OUR CUSTOMERS' HIGHEST-RATED FAVOURITES.

INTRODUCTION

'What's for dinner?' is the question on everyone's minds as the hours draw closer to dinnertime. Our recipes and our ingredients are designed to help make the answer easy — we love creating delicious yet quick recipes to be enjoyed during a busy week.

It's rewarding to know that so many families, couples and individuals throughout New Zealand and Australia are cooking and enjoying our goodness. We love that our recipes and our ingredients are being shared around the table, that our recipes are teaching children cooking skills and that people feel we're helping to make healthier, delicious, seasonal food accessible and easy. Nothing's more motivating than that!

This is our second cookbook and, like the first it is crammed full of our customers' highest-rated favourites. All of our recipes are a collaboration: the perfect blend of your feedback mixed with recipe testing and tweaking by our team of chefs and nutritionists. Your calls, emails and messages help connect us to each of you. All the time we're trying to make our recipes more delicious and easy, and your feedback is always taken on board — we deliver the goodness, the wow factor and the perfect amount of zing every night.

We've divided this book into four colourful sections, to make it a little easier to find a yummy recipe to perfectly fit the season, from a warming winter soup to a summer barbecue. Our recipes are easy to follow, with few steps and a clear indication of time; even the smallest family member or most junior foodie will be able to learn and grow in the kitchen, gaining skills and knowledge for the future.

At the heart of all our recipes is Nadia's Nude Food philosophy. Less cheeky than it sounds, Nude Food is all about stripping food back to the basics and ignoring the fads and media hype around how we should or shouldn't be eating. Nude Food is about eating naturally, with ingredients straight from the sea, the land and the sky. Food kept simple and fresh and less tampered with. It is this philosophy that guides our choice of ingredients and suppliers as well as the recipe design for our Food Bags. We like to think of this as good food, instinctively. It's all focused on the best produce from each season, free-range, sustainably farmed and locally grown.

Every week we deliver recipes just like these ones, with all of the ingredients required, so families, couples and individuals can enjoy tasty and nutritionally balanced meals. If you haven't yet tried My Food Bag, we'd love you to give it a go! On the front flap you'll find a special promotional code that will give you a taste of our goodness with recipes just like these, and all of the ingredients delivered to your door.

We hope that through this cookbook you'll never get stuck answering the 'what's for dinner?' question again.

Happy cooking and eating!
The My Food Bag team

MY FRESH
SPRING
RECIPES

THAI PORK PATTIES WITH COCONUT RICE AND CUCUMBER RADISH SALAD

SERVES 4–5
READY IN: 35 MINUTES
PREP TIME: 20 MINUTES
COOK TIME: 20 MINUTES

THAI PORK PATTIES

600g pork mince
1 teaspoon salt
2 teaspoons finely grated ginger
1 tablespoon sesame oil
1½ tablespoons sweet chilli sauce
1 teaspoon fish sauce
2 kaffir lime leaves, central stem
   removed, leaves very finely sliced
¼ cup chopped coriander leaves
2 spring onions, white part only
   (reserve green part for garnish),
   finely sliced then roughly chopped
1 egg
1 cup panko breadcrumbs

CUCUMBER RADISH SALAD

½ telegraph cucumber
2–3 handfuls mung bean sprouts
2 spring onions, green part only,
   finely sliced
3 baby radishes, thinly sliced
100g snow peas, tips and stringy bit
   removed, finely sliced
¼ cup torn coriander leaves

DRESSING

2 teaspoons runny honey
1½ tablespoons lemon juice
½ teaspoon fish sauce
1½ teaspoons sesame oil
3 tablespoons olive oil
¼ teaspoon salt

TO SERVE

steamed coconut rice (see page 176)
extra torn coriander leaves and
   sliced spring onion
1 lime, cut into weges

1 Start by making the coconut rice. While rice is cooking, combine all Thai pork patty ingredients in a large bowl and mix well, using your hands. Divide mixture and roll into 8–10 balls then flatten slightly. Heat a drizzle of oil in a large fry-pan on low to medium heat and cook patties in batches for 2–3 minutes each side until golden brown and cooked through. Take care not to let patties burn.

2 While patties cook, prepare salad. Peel cucumber on all sides into long ribbons, stopping when you reach the centre seeds. Finely chop the cucumber centre and combine in a large bowl with cucumber ribbons, mung bean sprouts, spring onions, radishes, snow peas and coriander.

3 Whisk all dressing ingredients together in a small bowl and toss with salad just prior to serving.

TO SERVE divide pork patties, rice and salad between plates and garnish with extra coriander and spring onion. Serve with lime wedges to squeeze over just before eating.

ENERGY	2838kJ (676kcal)
CARBOHYDRATE	58.9g
PROTEIN	35.6g
FAT	35.5g

   use GF breadcrumbs

> "Another delicious meal. Loved the coconut flavour of the rice. The cucumber salad was very simple, but also so flavoursome."
>
> SANDRA

> "Ten out of ten! Was gobbled up by everyone — even my three-year-old scoffed the beans."
>
> EMMA

BEAN AND VEGETABLE NACHOS

SERVES 4–5
READY IN: 25 MINUTES
PREP TIME: 10 MINUTES
COOK TIME: 20 MINUTES

BEAN AND VEGETABLE SAUCE

1 tablespoon oil
1 onion, grated or finely diced
1 teaspoon ground cumin
1 teaspoon ground coriander
2 carrots, peeled and grated
1 courgette, grated
1 red, yellow or orange capsicum,
   core and seeds removed, finely
   diced
1 red chilli, seeds removed and
   finely chopped (optional)
1 teaspoon cocoa powder
1 x 400g can mild chilli beans
1 x 400g can chopped tomatoes
¾ cup grated cheese (e.g. edam,
   colby or tasty)

GUACAMOLE

flesh of 1 ripe avocado
1–2 tablespoons lemon or lime juice

TO SERVE

200g good-quality corn chips
½ cup sour cream
½ iceberg or 1 cos lettuce, finely
   shredded
¼ cup chopped coriander leaves
½ lemon or 1 lime, cut into wedges

PREHEAT oven grill to high.

1 Heat oil in a large fry-pan (preferably oven-proof) on medium heat. Cook onion for 3–4 minutes until golden. Add cumin, coriander, carrots, courgette, capsicum and chilli (if using) and cook a further 4–5 minutes until vegetables are soft. Add a splash of water if vegetables or spices start to stick.

2 Stir in cocoa, chilli beans and canned tomatoes. Simmer for about 5 minutes until sauce has thickened slightly. Season to taste with salt and pepper. Sprinkle over cheese and grill for 2–3 minutes until cheese is golden. If you are not using an oven-proof pan, transfer mixture to a large casserole dish before topping with cheese and grilling.

3 In a small bowl, mash avocado with lemon or lime juice and season to taste with salt and pepper.

TO SERVE place a handful of corn chips into each bowl and spoon over bean and vegetable mixture. Top with a dollop of sour cream and guacamole, some lettuce and coriander. Squeeze over a wedge of lemon or lime just before eating.

ENERGY	2587kJ (616kcal)
CARBOHYDRATE	53.3g
PROTEIN	17.3g
FAT	35.2g

    omit cheese and sour cream

LEMONGRASS GRILLED CHICKEN WITH GREEN BEAN AND RICE NOODLE SALAD

SERVES 4–5
READY IN: 35 MINUTES
PREP TIME: 15 MINUTES
COOK TIME: 20 MINUTES

LEMONGRASS GRILLED CHICKEN

6 tablespoons lemongrass
   marinade (see page 176)
600g boneless, skinless chicken
   breasts or thighs, diced 3cm
12 bamboo skewers, soaked in
   water for 10 minutes

GREEN BEAN AND RICE NOODLE SALAD

200g dried rice stick noodles
½ cup roasted salted peanuts,
   roughly chopped
3 baby bok choy or Shanghai pak
   choy, rinsed, leaves and stalks
   finely sliced
200g green beans, trimmed, very
   thinly sliced
2 spring onions, finely sliced
½ telegraph cucumber, halved
   lengthways, thinly sliced on an
   angle
½ cup roughly chopped Thai herbs
   (e.g. coriander, mint, Thai basil
   and Vietnamese mint)
3 handfuls mung bean sprouts

DRESSING

6 tablespoons lime or lemon juice
3 tablespoons fish sauce or soy
   sauce
3 tablespoons sweet chilli sauce
1 kaffir lime leaf, tough central stem
   removed, leaves very finely
   sliced

TO SERVE

1 red chilli, finely sliced (optional)
1 lime, cut into wedges

PREHEAT BBQ grill to medium (if using). Bring a medium-sized pot of water to the boil.

1 Start by making the lemongrass marinade (see page 176).

2 Combine chicken with lemongrass paste and leave to marinate at room temperature for 5–10 minutes while you prepare the rest of the meal.

3 Cook noodles in a pot of boiling water until soft, about 3 minutes, or according to packet instructions. Drain and run under cold water to prevent noodles sticking. Use scissors to snip noodles in a few places to shorten strands. In a small bowl, mix all dressing ingredients together and set aside.

4 Thread marinated chicken onto bamboo skewers and season with salt. Heat a drizzle of oil in a large grill pan or fry-pan on medium heat (or use BBQ grill). Cook chicken skewers for about 2 minutes on all four sides, or until cooked through.

5 Toss noodles with peanuts, bok choy, beans, spring onions, cucumber, herbs, mung bean sprouts and dressing.

TO SERVE divide noodle salad between plates and top with lemongrass chicken skewers. Garnish with chilli (if using) and serve with lime wedges.

ENERGY	2264kJ (539kcal)
CARBOHYDRATE	54.8g
PROTEIN	42.0g
FAT	16.7g

    use GF soy sauce

LEMON 'N' PARSLEY FISH NUGGETS WITH KALE SLAW AND VEGGIE CHIPS

SERVES 4–5
READY IN: 40 MINUTES
PREP TIME: 25 MINUTES
COOK TIME: 25 MINUTES

VEGGIE CHIPS

400g agria potatoes, scrubbed (leave skin on) and cut into 1cm thick chips
300g red, orange or golden kumara, scrubbed (leave skin on) and cut into 1cm thick chips
3 carrots, cut into 2cm wide batons

KALE SLAW

¼ cup natural unsweetened yoghurt
¼ cup mayonnaise
4 teaspoons lemon juice
2–3 teaspoons vinegar (e.g. red wine, white wine, cider)
3–4 cups finely shredded green cabbage
100g curly kale, leaves stripped from tough stalk, very finely sliced
2 red apples, grated

LEMON 'N' PARSLEY FISH NUGGETS

2 ¼ cups panko breadcrumbs
zest of 1 lemon
¼ cup chopped parsley
2 eggs
¼ cup milk
½ cup flour
¾ teaspoon salt
600g boneless, skinless white fish fillets

TO SERVE

1 lemon, cut into wedges
tomato sauce (optional)

PREHEAT oven to 220°C. Line two oven trays with baking paper.

1 Place potatoes, kumara and carrots on prepared trays, toss with a drizzle of olive oil and season with salt and pepper. Bake for about 25 minutes or until tender and golden. Turn once during cooking.

2 While chips are cooking, prepare slaw. Mix yoghurt, mayonnaise, lemon juice and vinegar together in a large bowl. Add cabbage, kale and apple and toss to combine. Set aside.

3 Mix breadcrumbs, lemon zest and parsley in a bowl. Whisk eggs and milk in another bowl. Season flour with salt in a third bowl. Pat fish dry and remove any remaining scales or bones. Cut into 4cm pieces. Toss fish pieces in flour. Dip a few pieces at a time in the egg mixture, followed by the breadcrumbs, shaking off any excess as you go. Repeat with remaining fish pieces and set aside on a clean, dry plate.

4 When veggie chips are nearly done, heat a drizzle of oil in a large fry-pan (preferably non-stick) on medium to high heat. Fry fish nuggets, in batches, until golden and cooked through, about 2 minutes each side. Add a little extra oil as required.

TO SERVE place veggie chips, slaw and fish nuggets onto plates. Serve with lemon wedges to squeeze over fish just before eating, and tomato sauce (if desired).

ENERGY	2556kJ (609kcal)
CARBOHYDRATE	73.7g
PROTEIN	38.8g
FAT	17.5g

 MED TIME · GLUTEN FREE use GF flour and breadcrumbs

MISO ORANGE GLAZED SALMON WITH EDAMAME QUINOA SALAD

SERVES 4–5
READY IN: 35 MINUTES
PREP TIME: 15 MINUTES
COOK TIME: 20 MINUTES

EDAMAME QUINOA SALAD

2 ¼ cups water
1 ½ cups quinoa
good pinch of salt
2 cups frozen, podded edamame beans, defrosted
1 bunch (4–5) baby radishes, ends trimmed, thinly sliced
2 spring onions, thinly sliced
2–3 handfuls watercress

MISO ORANGE GLAZED SALMON

⅔ cup freshly squeezed orange juice
1 tablespoon sugar
⅓ cup water
2 tablespoons mirin or white wine
3 tablespoons white miso paste (see page 180)
600g salmon fillet (skin on), cut into 4–5 pieces

DRESSING

2 teaspoons soy sauce
2 teaspoons sesame oil
1 teaspoon sugar
2 tablespoons lemon juice
1 tablespoon extra virgin olive oil
2 teaspoons mirin or white wine

TO SERVE

1–2 tablespoons toasted sesame seeds*

1 Bring water to the boil in a medium pot (with a tight-fitting lid). As soon as it boils, stir in quinoa and salt. Cover with lid and reduce to lowest heat to cook for 12 minutes. Turn off heat and leave to steam, still covered, for a further 8 minutes. Do not lift lid at any time during cooking.

2 While quinoa cooks, prepare glaze. In a small bowl, mix orange juice, sugar, water, mirin or white wine and miso paste together and set aside.

3 Bring a small pot of salted water to the boil and cook edamame beans for 2–3 minutes or until cooked. Refresh under cold water.

4 In a small bowl, combine all dressing ingredients and set aside.

5 Pat salmon dry with paper towels, remove any remaining pin bones and season with salt. Heat a drizzle of oil in a large fry-pan on medium to high heat. Cook salmon, skin-side down, until skin is golden and crisp, 2–3 minutes. Flip salmon over, reduce heat to medium and add miso orange glaze. The glaze will simmer rapidly and thicken in the fry-pan. Baste salmon with glaze and continue to cook for a further 2 minutes for medium or until cooked to your liking. If you find the glaze is getting too thick, add 1–2 tablespoons water as required.

6 Combine quinoa, edamame, radishes, spring onions and watercress with dressing just before serving.

TO SERVE divide edamame quinoa salad between plates. Place salmon on top, spoon over remaining glaze and sprinkle with sesame seeds.

*TIP
Toast sesame seeds in a small, dry fry-pan on medium heat for 30–60 seconds until light golden, moving pan frequently to avoid burning.

ENERGY	2869kJ (683kcal)
CARBOHYDRATE	50.6g
PROTEIN	46.4g
FAT	32.0g

"Delicious taste explosions.
Miso orange glaze, wow!
Dressing for edamame
beans fab."

CHICKEN AND BEAN QUESADILLAS, AVOCADO SALSA AND CHIPOTLE SOUR CREAM

SERVES 4–5
READY IN: 50 MINUTES
PREP TIME: 25 MINUTES
COOK TIME: 25 MINUTES

CHICKEN AND BEAN QUESADILLAS

¾ red onion, finely diced
1 clove garlic, minced
½ red chilli, seeds removed and finely chopped (optional)
500g boneless, skinless chicken breasts or thighs
1 tablespoon Mexican spice mix (see page 177)
1 x 400g can beans (e.g. pinto, black, cannellini, kidney), drained and rinsed
½ cup tomato passata or canned, crushed tomatoes
1 cup grated cheese (e.g. tasty, colby, edam)
10 medium, soft, plain wheat or corn tortilla wraps
2 tablespoons chipotle sauce (store-bought)

AVOCADO TOMATO SALSA

flesh of 1 firm-ripe avocado, diced
2 tomatoes, diced
¼ red onion, finely diced
½ red chilli, finely chopped (optional)
¼ cup chopped coriander leaves
1 tablespoon lime or lemon juice

CHIPOTLE SOUR CREAM

½ cup sour cream or natural unsweetened Greek yoghurt
2 tablespoons chipotle sauce (store-bought)

TO SERVE

½ iceberg or 1 cos lettuce, finely shredded
¼ cup chopped coriander leaves
1 lime, cut into wedges

PREHEAT oven to 100°C. Place a large baking tray in oven.

1 Heat a drizzle of oil in a large fry-pan on medium heat. Cook onion, garlic and chilli (if using) for 3–4 minutes until soft. Remove from pan and set aside. Wipe out pan with a paper towel.

2 Pat chicken dry with paper towels and cut into 2–3cm strips. Coat with Mexican spice mix and season with salt. Add another drizzle of oil to same pan and cook chicken, in batches, for 3–4 minutes until just cooked through. Remove from pan and roughly chop into smaller pieces (about 0.5cm). In a medium bowl, mix together chicken, onion mixture, beans, passata or crushed tomatoes and cheese.

3 Place a tortilla wrap on bench and spoon ½–¾ cup chicken mixture on top. Spread out to cover tortilla, leaving a 1cm gap around the edge. Drizzle with some chipotle sauce, then top with another tortilla. Repeat with remaining tortillas and chicken mixture.

4 In a medium bowl, combine all avocado tomato salsa ingredients together and season with salt and pepper.

5 Heat a drizzle of oil in a large fry-pan on medium heat. Fry each quesadilla until golden and crispy, about 1 minute each side. Push down on the quesadilla with a fish slice as you fry it, to flatten it slightly. Transfer to tray in oven to keep warm while you fry remaining quesadillas.

6 In a small bowl, mix sour cream or yoghurt and chipotle sauce together.

TO SERVE cut each quesadilla into wedges. Pile onto a big chopping board and serve with lettuce and salsa. Dollop over chipotle sour cream and garnish with coriander. Squeeze over lime juice just before eating.

ENERGY	2242kJ (534kcal)	
CARBOHYDRATE	42.6g	
PROTEIN	39.4g	
FAT	23.4g	

 MORE TIME · GLUTEN FREE · use GF corn tortilla wraps

PASTA WITH SUNDRIED TOMATO, COURGETTE AND BACON CREAM SAUCE

SERVES 5
READY IN: 30 MINUTES
PREP TIME: 15 MINUTES
COOK TIME: 15 MINUTES

SAUCE AND PASTA

250g bacon (e.g. streaky or short loin), diced 1 cm

3 courgettes, grated

100g sundried tomato pesto (store-bought or see page 178)

¾ cup chicken stock

½ cup cream

400g fresh or dried pasta (e.g. fusilli, rigatoni etc)

¼ cup sliced basil leaves

SALAD

1 cos lettuce, roughly chopped

½ telegraph cucumber, diced

flesh of 1 firm-ripe avocado, diced

1 red, yellow or orange capsicum, core and seeds removed, thinly sliced

red wine vinegar dressing or honey mustard dressing (see page 179)

TO SERVE

¼ cup basil leaves

¼ cup shaved parmesan cheese

BRING a large pot of salted water to the boil.

1 Heat a drizzle of oil in a large fry-pan on high heat. Add bacon and cook for 3 minutes until starting to become golden. Reduce heat to medium, add courgettes and cook for a further minute until softened. Stir in sundried tomato pesto, chicken stock and cream. Bring to a simmer, then simmer gently on low heat for 1 minute. Turn off and set aside.

2 Cook pasta in pot of boiling water for about 8 minutes (or according to packet instructions) until al dente (just tender).

3 Toss all salad ingredients together.

4 Drain pasta then add to pan with the sauce along with basil. Reheat sauce on a low heat until warmed through, about 2 minutes. Season to taste with salt and pepper.

TO SERVE spoon pasta into bowls and scatter over extra basil leaves and parmesan. Serve with salad on the side.

ENERGY	2774kJ (660kcal)
CARBOHYDRATE	57.5g
PROTEIN	27.7g
FAT	35.1g

MED TIME

> "
> We are big pasta
> lovers and this dish
> was awesome! Heaps
> of flavour and so
> super tasty. "
> CARLA

"Outstanding —
never thought
cauliflower could
taste this good!"
GWYNETH

GRILLED CHICKEN WITH CRUNCHY CAULIFLOWER, ORANGE AND ALMOND SALAD

SERVES 4–5
READY IN: 30 MINUTES
PREP TIME: 15–20 MINUTES
COOK TIME: 15 MINUTES

GRILLED CHICKEN

600g boneless, skinless chicken
  breasts
1 tablespoon olive oil
1 tablespoon finely chopped
  thyme leaves
2 cloves garlic, minced
2 tablespoons lemon juice

CAULIFLOWER, ORANGE AND ALMOND SALAD

1 head cauliflower, finely chopped
  until you have 5–6 cups
2 tablespoons olive oil
¾ teaspoon fennel seeds
¾ teaspoon cumin seeds
4 cloves garlic, minced
1 punnet cherry tomatoes, cut in half
½ red onion, very thinly sliced
2 oranges, peeled and cut into
  segments (reserve zest to serve)
zest and juice of 1½ lemons
1–2 tablespoons extra virgin
  olive oil
¼ cup chopped coriander leaves
¼ cup chopped flat-leaf
  parsley leaves
60g feta cheese, crumbled
½ cup toasted, sliced almonds*

TO SERVE

zest of 1 orange
2 tablespoons chopped
  flat-leaf parsley leaves

BRING a full kettle to the boil. Preheat BBQ grill to high (if using).

1 Pat chicken dry with paper towels and cut into steaks. To do this, place your hand flat on top of each chicken breast and use a knife to slice through horizontally to make 2 thin steaks, trying to keep each side an equal thickness. In a large dish, combine chicken with olive oil, thyme, garlic and lemon juice and leave to marinate while you prepare rest of meal.

2 Place cauliflower in a large, heat-proof bowl and pour over boiling water to cover. Leave for 1 minute then drain well.

3 Add olive oil to same pan and fry fennel and cumin seeds and garlic for about 30 seconds. Add drained cauliflower and toss with spices and garlic for a further 1–2 minutes. The cauliflower should retain its crunch. Place aside in a large mixing bowl with all remaining salad ingredients, and gently toss to combine. Season to taste with salt and freshly ground black pepper.

4 Heat same pan to medium to high heat (or use BBQ grill). Season chicken with salt and cook, in batches, for 2–3 minutes each side until cooked through. Set aside, covered with foil, to rest for a few minutes then slice.

TO SERVE divide salad and chicken between plates. Scatter over orange zest and parsley.

*TIP
Toast almonds in a small, dry fry-pan on medium heat for 1-2 minutes until golden, moving pan frequently to avoid burning.

ENERGY	2037kJ (485kcal)
CARBOHYDRATE	15.3g
PROTEIN	39.6g
FAT	28.8g

    omit feta

FENNEL-DUSTED FISH WITH ROASTED CARROTS, FARRO AND LEMON CRÈME FRAÎCHE

SERVES 4–5
READY IN: 35 MINUTES
PREP TIME: 15 MINUTES
COOK TIME: 20 MINUTES

FARRO
1¼ cups farro
1 cup raisins

LEMON CRÈME FRAÎCHE
1 cup crème fraîche
zest and juice of 1 lemon

ROASTED CARROTS
2 bunches baby carrots, scrubbed
   and ends trimmed (leave a little
   green stem)
2 onions, diced
½ teaspoon ground cardamom
½ teaspoon ground cumin
½ teaspoon brown sugar
¼ teaspoon dried rosemary
knob of butter
2 teaspoons runny honey
3–4 handfuls rocket leaves

FENNEL-DUSTED FISH
600g boneless, skinless white
   fish fillets
2 teaspoons cornflour
2 teaspoons ground fennel
1 teaspoon freshly ground black
   pepper
1 tablespoon chopped thyme
   leaves
2 tablespoons butter

TO SERVE
1 lemon, cut into wedges

PREHEAT oven to 220°C. Line an oven tray with baking paper. Bring a large pot of salted water to the boil.

1 Cook farro in pot of boiling water for 20 minutes until just cooked, but still slightly chewy. Add raisins for the last minute of cook time. Drain, rinse under cold water, then drain again thoroughly. In a small bowl combine crème fraîche, lemon zest and juice and mix well.

2 Place carrots and onions on prepared tray and toss with remaining roasted vegetable ingredients (except rocket leaves) and a drizzle of olive oil. Season with salt and pepper and roast for 16–18 minutes until golden. Turn once during cooking.

3 Pat fish dry with paper towels, removing any remaining scales or bones. On a plate, combine cornflour, fennel, pepper and thyme. Season fish with salt and dust on both sides with cornflour mixture. Heat butter and a drizzle of oil in a large fry-pan (preferably non-stick) on medium to high heat. Cook fish for about 2 minutes each side until golden brown and just cooked through. Set aside and cover to keep warm.

4 In a large bowl, combine cooked farro and raisins with roasted vegetables and rocket, and season with salt and pepper. Fold through half the lemon crème fraîche.

TO SERVE spoon farro and vegetables onto each plate with a piece of fish. Squeeze over lemon juice and drizzle with remaining lemon crème fraîche.

ENERGY	2527kJ (602kcal)
CARBOHYDRATE	66.2g
PROTEIN	35.7g
FAT	20.8g

 MED TIME DAIRY FREE omit crème fraîche and butter

“Such an interesting and unexpected combo of flavours that really worked well. Very easy too.”
VICTORIA

"A huge hit and very tasty for lunch the next day — even the fussy seven-year-old loved them."

SUE

PORK, APPLE, VEGETABLE AND CRANBERRY FILO ROLLS WITH SPRING VEG

SERVES 4–5
READY IN: 50 MINUTES
PREP TIME: 25 MINUTES
COOK TIME: 30 MINUTES

PORK, APPLE, VEGETABLE AND CRANBERRY FILO ROLLS

1 onion, finely diced
1 courgette, grated
2 carrots, peeled and grated
1 apple, core removed and grated
  (squeeze out excess moisture)
½ teaspoon salt
600g pork sausage meat (buy
  good-quality raw sausages
  and squeeze the meat out of
  the casings)
¼ cup dried cranberries, roughly
  chopped
¾ cup panko breadcrumbs
15 sheets filo pastry
1–2 tablespoons olive oil,
  melted butter or olive oil spray,
  for brushing
1 tablespoon sesame seeds

SPRING VEG

1 bunch asparagus (about 12
  spears), trimmed
250g snow peas or sugar snaps,
  tips and stringy bit removed
3–4 tablespoons red wine vinegar
  dressing (see page 179)

TO SERVE

tomato sauce or chutney (optional)

PREHEAT oven to 200°C. Line an oven tray with baking paper.

1 Heat a drizzle of oil in a large fry-pan on medium heat and cook onion, courgette, carrots, apple and salt until soft, 6–8 minutes. Allow to cool slightly. To speed up this process, spread onto a dish and place in the fridge for 10 minutes.

2 Place pork sausage meat, cooked vegetables, cranberries and panko breadcrumbs in a large bowl. Season well with salt and pepper. Using clean hands mix until well combined. Divide mixture into 10 portions, using a half cup measure. Place 1 sheet of filo on a clean bench with the long edge facing you. Brush (or spray) with olive oil or butter and place another 2 sheets on top.

3 Cut filo in half vertically. Put 1 measure of sausage mixture onto each piece on the bottom half. Shape mixture into a sausage, allowing a 2cm border at the edges. Roll filo over once, tuck in the sides and roll up into a tight parcel.

4 Repeat to make a total of 10 parcels. Place on prepared tray, seam-side-down. Brush or spray with olive oil or butter and sprinkle with sesame seeds. Bake for about 20 minutes or until golden and cooked through.

5 While sausage rolls are cooking, bring a medium pot of salted water to the boil. Add asparagus and snow peas to pot of boiling water and cook for 1–2 minutes until bright green and tender. Drain then toss with dressing just before serving.

TO SERVE place 1–2 filo rolls on each plate and serve spring veg on the side. Add a dollop of tomato sauce or chutney (if using).

ENERGY	2617kJ (623kcal)
CARBOHYDRATE	71.01g
PROTEIN	36.2g
FAT	19.8g

 use oil instead of butter

HERB-CRUSTED LAMB WITH ROAST POTATO AND ASPARAGUS SALAD

SERVES 4—5
READY IN: 45 MINUTES
PREP TIME: 20 MINUTES
COOK TIME: 30 MINUTES

ROAST POTATO SALAD

800g red jacket or agria potatoes, scrubbed (leave skin on) and diced 3–4cm
1 tablespoon olive oil
2 bunches asparagus spears (about 24 spears), ends trimmed, cut into 4cm lengths
2 courgettes, ends trimmed and sliced 1cm on an angle
1 punnet cherry tomatoes, cut in half
¼ cup chopped mint leaves
½ red onion, finely diced
100g feta cheese, crumbled

HERB-CRUSTED LAMB

600g lamb loin or lamb rump steaks (at room temperature)
2 tablespoons finely chopped rosemary leaves
2 tablespoons finely chopped mint leaves
1 cup panko breadcrumbs
2 tablespoons olive oil
3 teaspoons Dijon mustard

PREHEAT oven to 200°C. Line two oven trays with baking paper.

1 Toss potatoes with olive oil on first prepared tray and season with salt and pepper. Bake for 30 minutes until golden and crispy. Turn once during cooking.

2 While potatoes are cooking, prepare lamb. Pat lamb dry with paper towels and season with salt. Heat a drizzle of oil in a large fry-pan on high heat and sear lamb for 1 minute each side until just brown (it will finish cooking in the oven). Place on second prepared tray. Mix herbs with breadcrumbs and olive oil in a small bowl. Spread mustard on top of each piece of lamb. Sprinkle crust mixture on top and press gently but firmly to adhere.

3 When potatoes have about 10 minutes of cooking time remaining, place lamb in oven (on rack above potatoes) and toss asparagus and courgettes through potatoes. Cook vegetables and lamb for about 8 minutes for medium rare (depending on thickness) or until cooked to your liking. Set lamb aside, loosely covered with foil, to rest for 5 minutes.

4 Add tomatoes, mint, onion and feta to tray with potatoes and vegetables and toss to combine. Drizzle with extra virgin olive oil and a little red wine vinegar then season to taste with salt and pepper. Slice lamb thickly.

TO SERVE divide lamb and salad between plates. If some of the crust falls off the lamb, just sprinkle it back on before serving.

ENERGY	2389kJ (569kcal)
CARBOHYDRATE	42.6g
PROTEIN	39.4g
FAT	26.1g

  omit feta   omit breadcrumbs or use GF breadcrumbs

"What neat taste combinations. A beautiful marriage of flavours!"

PIERRE

Loved the crisp, clean flavours of this dish. Everything worked so well together and we fought over the leftovers for lunch."

NICOLA

MACAROON-CRUSTED FISH WITH FRIES AND SPRING SLAW

SERVES 4–5
READY IN: 45 MINUTES
PREP TIME: 15 MINUTES
COOK TIME: 35 MINUTES

FRIES

800g agria potatoes, scrubbed
    (leave skin on) and cut into 1–2cm
    thick fries
1 tablespoon olive oil
1 tablespoon melted butter

MACAROON-CRUSTED FISH

½ cup ground almonds
½ cup desiccated coconut
4 teaspoons olive oil
zest of 1 lemon
600g boneless, skinless white
    fish fillets

SPRING SLAW

1 green or red apple, core
    removed, thinly sliced and cut into
    thin matchsticks
3–4 baby radishes, thinly sliced
    and cut into thin matchsticks
1 courgette, coarsely grated or cut
    into thin matchsticks
1 bunch asparagus (about 12
    spears) or green beans, trimmed
    and thinly sliced
½ red onion, finely sliced
juice of 1 lemon

TO SERVE

½ cup tartare sauce (store-bought
    or see page 178)

PREHEAT oven to 200°C. Line two oven trays with baking paper.

1 Toss potatoes with oil and butter on first prepared tray. Season with salt and pepper and bake for 30–35 minutes until golden. Turn once during cooking.

2 In a medium bowl, combine ground almonds, coconut, olive oil and lemon zest, mixing well. Pat fish fillets dry with paper towels and remove any remaining scales or bones. Lay fish on second prepared tray, season with salt and pepper and drizzle with a little oil. Lightly pack coconut mixture on top of each fillet. Bake until fish is cooked through, 10–12 minutes.

3 Combine all spring slaw ingredients in a medium bowl and mix well.

TO SERVE place a piece of fish and a handful of fries on each plate with slaw on the side. Serve with tartare sauce.

ENERGY	2646kJ (630kcal)
CARBOHYDRATE	37.8g
PROTEIN	32.7g
FAT	37.8g

   use oil instead of butter

PANANG FISH AND VEGETABLE CURRY

SERVES 4–5
READY IN: 30 MINUTES
PREP TIME: 10 MINUTES
COOK TIME: 20 MINUTES

**PANANG FISH AND
VEGETABLE CURRY**

1 tablespoon oil
2 shallots or ½ onion, finely diced
1 clove garlic, minced
1 teaspoon finely grated ginger
2 tablespoons store-bought
   panang curry paste or ¼ cup
   homemade panang curry paste
   (see page 178)
1 x 425ml can coconut milk
1 bunch broccolini, stalks trimmed
½ cup fish or chicken stock
2 tablespoons fish sauce
1–2 tablespoons brown sugar
600g boneless, skinless firm white
   fish fillets
1 red capsicum, core and seeds
   removed, thinly sliced
150g snow peas or sugar snaps,
   tips and stringy bit removed
juice of 1 lime

TO SERVE

steamed jasmine or basmati rice
   (see page 176)
¼ cup chopped coriander leaves
1 lime, cut into wedges

1 Start by cooking rice to serve with the meal. While rice is cooking, prepare curry. Heat oil in a large pot on medium heat. Add shallots or onion, garlic and ginger and cook for 1–2 minutes, until softened. Add curry paste and a few tablespoons of coconut milk, and continue cooking, while stirring, for 1–2 minutes. Add broccolini, remaining coconut milk, stock, fish sauce and sugar. Bring to a simmer, reduce heat to low and simmer for about 2 minutes.

2 Pat fish dry with paper towels, remove any remaining scales or bones and cut into 3cm pieces. Add fish and capsicum to curry and stir gently to combine.

3 Simmer on very low heat for 1–2 minutes or until fish is just cooked through. Stir through snow peas or sugar snaps and lime juice. Season to taste with extra fish sauce and brown sugar (if required).

TO SERVE place rice and curry, garnished with coriander, in large serving bowls, for people to help themselves. Squeeze over extra lime juice just before serving.

ENERGY	2292kJ (546kcal)
CARBOHYDRATE	53.5g
PROTEIN	33.1g
FAT	22.4g

MED TIME · DAIRY FREE · GLUTEN FREE

> Full of flavour. The veges make a wonderful crunchy contrast to the firm fish and the sauce was creamy with just the right amount of bite."

JACQUI

"
Very tasty and
straightforward."
RHIANNON

LAMB AND VEGETABLE KEBABS WITH WARM POTATO SALAD AND GRILLED ASPARAGUS

SERVES 4–5
READY IN: 45 MINUTES
PREP TIME: 20 MINUTES
COOK TIME: 25 MINUTES

WARM POTATO SALAD
800g baby potatoes
¼ cup creamy dressing (see page 179)
¼ cup chopped flat-leaf parsley leaves
30g gherkins, roughly chopped
2 stalks celery, thinly sliced

LAMB AND VEGETABLE KEBABS
600g lamb rumps (at room temperature), diced 2–3cm
1 red onion, diced 2–3cm
2 capsicums (red and yellow), diced 2cm
12 bamboo skewers, soaked in water for 10 minutes
2 tablespoons finely chopped thyme leaves
2 tablespoons olive oil

GRILLED ASPARAGUS
2 bunches asparagus spears (about 24 spears), trimmed

TO SERVE
tomato chutney or relish (optional)

BRING a large pot of salted water to the boil. Preheat BBQ grill to high (if using).

1 Cook potatoes in boiling salted water until tender, 10–12 minutes.

2 While potatoes are cooking, assemble kebabs. Thread a piece of lamb, onion and each colour capsicum onto each skewer, repeating until you have 3–4 pieces of lamb on each skewer. Place kebabs in a dish, sprinkle with thyme, drizzle with olive oil and season with salt and pepper.

3 Heat a large fry-pan on high heat. Cook kebabs, in batches, for 1–2 minutes on all four sides for medium-rare or until cooked to your liking. Set aside to rest for 2–3 minutes. Add a drizzle of oil to pan and cook asparagus until lightly charred, about 2 minutes. Alternatively cook kebabs and asparagus on BBQ.

4 In a large bowl, whisk creamy dressing ingredients together, then stir through parsley, gherkins and celery. Season to taste with salt and pepper. Drain potatoes and gently toss through.

TO SERVE spoon some warm potato salad and grilled asparagus onto each plate. Serve with a few lamb and vegetable kebabs and tomato chutney or relish if using.

ENERGY	1966kJ (468kcal)
CARBOHYDRATE	35.7g
PROTEIN	34.3g
FAT	20.3g

    omit yoghurt from creamy dressing

CHICKEN WITH MASHED POTATO, ROCKET, ASPARAGUS AND PANCETTA

SERVES 4–5
READY IN: 35 MINUTES
PREP TIME: 15 MINUTES
COOK TIME: 20 MINUTES

MASHED POTATO

800g agria potatoes, peeled and
  chopped
2 tablespoons smoked butter
  (just use regular butter if you can't
  find smoked)
¼ cup milk

CHICKEN

600g boneless, skinless chicken
  breasts
¼ cup chicken stock
1 tablespoon finely chopped
  rosemary leaves

ROCKET, ASPARAGUS
AND PANCETTA

100g pancetta or bacon,
  finely sliced
2 shallots, finely diced
2 cloves garlic, minced
2 bunches asparagus spears
  (about 24 spears), trimmed
¼ cup chicken stock
2 teaspoons smoked butter
  (just use regular butter if you
  can't find smoked)
1 tablespoon red wine vinegar
pinch of chilli flakes (optional)
120–150g rocket leaves

PREHEAT oven to 200°C. Bring a large pot of salted water to the boil.

1 Cook potatoes in pot of boiling water until very soft, 12–15 minutes. Drain and mash with butter and milk. Season to taste with salt and pepper, and keep warm.

2 Heat a drizzle of olive oil in a large fry-pan on medium to high heat. Pat chicken dry with paper towels and season with salt and pepper. Cook for 2–3 minutes each side until browned. Transfer to a small baking dish, pour over chicken stock and sprinkle with rosemary. Bake until cooked through, 10–12 minutes (depending on thickness). Set aside, covered in foil, to rest for 5 minutes. Then slice on an angle.

3 Return same pan to medium heat with a drizzle of oil. Cook pancetta or bacon until starting to become crispy, about 1 minute. Add shallots and garlic and cook until just soft, about 2 minutes. Remove from pan and set aside, keeping pan on heat. Fry asparagus until bright green, 1–2 minutes. Add chicken stock, butter, vinegar, chilli flakes (if using) and pancetta/shallot mix. Toss to combine. Add rocket leaves and stir to combine just before serving.

TO SERVE spoon some mash and rocket, asparagus and pancetta onto each plate. Top with slices of chicken and spoon over any remaining sauce from the chicken dish.

ENERGY	1804kJ (430kcal)
CARBOHYDRATE	32.2g
PROTEIN	41.4g
FAT	14.3g

"
Yummy flavours. Delicious,
flavour-filled, juicy patties and
lovely fresh salad. Enjoyed the
sweet cranberry sauce too."
ROBYN

TURKEY BURGERS WITH CRANBERRY SAUCE AND RAW ENERGY SALAD

SERVES 4–5
READY IN: 40 MINUTES
PREP TIME: 20 MINUTES
COOK TIME: 20 MINUTES

TURKEY BURGERS

600g turkey mince (or use chicken
  mince if you can't find turkey)
¾ red onion, very finely diced
1 clove garlic, minced
1 teaspoon lemon pepper
1 teaspoon paprika
½ teaspoon ground turmeric
1 teaspoon dried oregano
1 egg
½ teaspoon salt
¼ teaspoon freshly ground black
  pepper
1 cup panko breadcrumbs
1 tablespoon Worcestershire sauce

RAW ENERGY SALAD

1 beetroot, peeled and grated
2 carrots, peeled and grated
¼ red onion, finely diced
¼ cup chopped parsley
¼ cup sunflower seeds
¼ cup dried cranberries
1 tablespoon extra virgin olive oil
1 tablespoon vinegar (e.g. red
  wine, white wine, cider)

TO SERVE

4–5 burger buns
100g cranberry sauce
  (store-bought)
¼ cup mayonnaise
1 small lettuce (e.g. baby cos or
  butterhead), leaves separated

PREHEAT oven to 200°C. Line an oven tray with baking paper.

1 Mix all turkey burger ingredients together in a large bowl, using your hands. Use a half cup measure to shape into 4–5 burger patties (about the size of a burger bun) and set aside on a tray in the fridge while you prepare the rest of the meal.

2 Place all raw energy salad ingredients in a large bowl and mix well. Season to taste with salt and pepper and set aside.

3 Slice the burger buns horizontally and place closed buns on prepared tray.

4 Heat a drizzle of oil in a large fry-pan (preferably non-stick) on low to medium heat and cook patties in batches for about 3 minutes each side until golden. Place on the same oven tray as buns, overlapping buns, if necessary, to fit. Bake for 5–8 minutes until patties are cooked through and buns are lightly toasted. You may need to remove buns after about 5 minutes.

TO SERVE dollop some cranberry sauce onto the base of each bun and top with a patty. Top with some mayonnaise and lettuce. Serve raw energy salad in the burger or on the side.

ENERGY	2909kJ (693kcal)
CARBOHYDRATE	71.3g
PROTEIN	43.0g
FAT	25.4g

DUCK BREAST WITH FIG SAUCE, ROASTED BEETROOT, KUMARA, FETA AND ROCKET

SERVES 4–5
READY IN: 35 MINUTES
PREP TIME: 15 MINUTES
COOK TIME: 20 MINUTES

ROASTED BEETROOT AND KUMARA

800g orange kumara, scrubbed
 (leave skin on) and diced 2cm
1 bunch baby beetroot, scrubbed
 (leave skin on) and cut into quarters

DUCK BREAST WITH FIG SAUCE

4 duck breasts (at room temperature)
2 shallots, finely diced
²/₃ cup red wine
¼ cup fig jam (store-bought, or use
 plum jam)
2 teaspoons butter
2 teaspoons lemon juice

TO SERVE

120g–150g rocket leaves
100g feta cheese

PREHEAT oven to 200°C. Line an oven tray with baking paper.

1 Toss kumara and beetroot with a drizzle of oil on prepared tray. Season with salt and pepper and roast for 20 minutes until soft. Turn once during cooking.

2 Trim duck breasts of overhanging excess fat. Use a sharp knife to score skin at 1cm intervals. Pat dry with paper towels and season with salt. Heat a large, dry fry-pan on medium heat. Cook duck, skin-side down, for 6–8 minutes until most of the fat has rendered out and skin is golden. If skin browns too quickly, reduce heat. Flip over and continue to cook for 4–5 minutes until duck is cooked through medium (it should be a pale, rosy pink inside, like medium-cooked lamb). Set aside, covered with foil, to rest for 5–10 minutes. Slice thinly on an angle.

3 Keep about 2 tablespoons of fat in the pan the duck was cooked in and discard the remainder, keeping pan on medium heat. Fry shallots until soft, 3–4 minutes. Add wine and reduce by half, about 2 minutes. Add fig jam and stir to melt, then turn off heat and stir through butter and lemon juice. Season to taste with salt and pepper. You may need to add a splash of water if the sauce becomes too sticky.

TO SERVE place a large handful of rocket on each plate. Top with roasted vegetables. Arrange duck on top of salad. Drizzle over fig sauce and crumble over feta. Sprinkle a few more rocket leaves on top if desired.

ENERGY	2421kJ (576kcal)
CARBOHYDRATE	61.3g
PROTEIN	34.8g
FAT	17.3g

   omit butter and feta

"
Loved the duck
with the fig sauce.
Super meal."
BARBARA

"
Delicious. We loved
the flavours and the
tangy citrus glaze.
Will definitely make
this again."
SUZANNE

ORANGE-GLAZED FISH WITH MOROCCAN COUSCOUS

SERVES 4–5
READY IN: 30 MINUTES
PREP TIME: 15 MINUTES
COOK TIME: 15 MINUTES

MOROCCAN COUSCOUS

1 tablespoon olive oil
1 red, yellow or orange capsicum, core and seeds removed, finely diced
1 red onion, finely diced
2 cloves garlic, finely chopped
¾ cup couscous
½ teaspoon salt
1 tablespoon olive oil
¾ cup boiling water
½ telegraph cucumber, diced
¼–½ cup chopped parsley
¼–½ cup chopped mint leaves
150g baby spinach leaves, roughly chopped
knob of butter
¼ cup dried currants
100g feta cheese, crumbled

ORANGE-GLAZED FISH

600g boneless, skinless white fish fillets
zest of 1 orange
juice of 2 oranges
1½–2 tablespoons butter

TO SERVE

¼ cup parsley and mint leaves

BRING a full kettle to the boil.

1 Heat olive oil in a medium fry-pan on medium-high heat. Cook capsicum, onion and garlic for about 3 minutes until slightly charred and onion is soft.

2 Place couscous, salt and olive oil in a medium, heat-proof bowl or pot and pour over boiling water. Mix with a fork then cover with a plate or lid and leave for 5–10 minutes until tender. Prepare cucumber, parsley, mint and spinach and place all in a large bowl.

3 Pat fish dry with paper towels, remove any remaining scales or bones and season with salt. Heat a drizzle of olive oil in a large fry-pan on medium to high heat. Fry fish for 1–2 minutes each side until just cooked through. Add orange zest and juice and butter in the last 30 seconds of cook time. Allow butter to melt then spoon orange-butter glaze over fish.

4 Add butter and currants to couscous and fluff up with a fork. Toss couscous with capsicum mixture, cucumber, herbs, spinach and feta. Season to taste with salt and pepper.

TO SERVE divide couscous between plates and top with a piece of fish. Spoon over any extra glaze from pan. Garnish with herbs.

ENERGY	1838kJ (438kcal)
CARBOHYDRATE	30.5g
PROTEIN	33.8g
FAT	19.9g

 MED TIME DAIRY FREE omit butter and feta

HARISSA CHICKEN AND VEGETABLE SKEWERS WITH QUINOA TABBOULEH

SERVES 4–5
READY IN: 40 MINUTES
PREP TIME: 20 MINUTES
COOK TIME: 20 MINUTES

QUINOA TABBOULEH

2 ¼ cups water
1 ½ cups quinoa
½ red onion, finely diced
2 tomatoes, diced 1cm
½ cup finely chopped parsley
   and mint leaves
2 tablespoons extra virgin olive oil
2 tablespoons vinegar (e.g. white
   wine, red wine)

HARISSA CHICKEN AND
VEGETABLE SKEWERS

600g chicken breasts, diced 2cm
¼ cup harissa marinade (see
   page 176)
2 courgettes, sliced 1cm
250g button mushrooms, sliced 1cm
12 bamboo skewers, soaked in
   water for 10 minutes

MINT AND CORIANDER
YOGHURT

1 cup natural unsweetened yoghurt
¼ cup chopped coriander leaves
¼ cup chopped mint leaves
juice of ½ lemon

PREHEAT BBQ hot plate to medium (if using).

1 Bring water to the boil in a medium pot on high heat. As soon as it boils, add quinoa and a pinch of salt. Cover with a tight-fitting lid and reduce to low heat and cook for 12 minutes. Turn off heat and leave to steam, still covered, for a further 8 minutes. Do not lift lid at any time during cooking.

2 While quinoa is cooking, combine chicken and harissa paste in a medium bowl. Gently toss to coat well. Thread a piece of chicken, courgette and mushroom onto each skewer and repeat until you have 3–4 pieces of each ingredient per skewer.

3 Heat a drizzle of olive oil in a large fry-pan or grill pan on medium heat (or use BBQ grill). Cook skewers for 1–2 minutes on all four sides until golden and chicken is cooked through. Reduce heat if they brown too quickly. Use a fish slice to gently press down on chicken while cooking to ensure even contact with pan. Set aside on a plate, covered with foil, to rest for 2–3 minutes.

4 Fluff up quinoa with a fork and transfer to a medium bowl with remaining quinoa tabbouleh ingredients. Mix and season to taste with salt and pepper.

5 In a small bowl mix yoghurt, coriander, mint and lemon juice together.

TO SERVE spoon some quinoa tabbouleh onto plates. Top with a few skewers and a dollop of mint and coriander yoghurt.

ENERGY	2227kJ (530kcal)
CARBOHYDRATE	37.6g
PROTEIN	43.2g
FAT	22.0g

    omit yoghurt

"These were a hit! Nicely spiced. The tabbouleh was good too."

TARINA

"
Loved the satay sauce!
Haven't tried marinated
tofu before but that was
yummy too."

LARRAINE

WARM GADO GADO SALAD WITH SATAY SAUCE

SERVES 5
READY IN: 45 MINUTES
PREP TIME: 25 MINUTES
COOK TIME: 20 MINUTES

TOFU AND MARINADE

300g firm tofu, thinly sliced
2 tablespoons sweet chilli sauce
1 tablespoon soy sauce
1 tablespoon finely grated ginger

SALAD

700–800g baby potatoes,
  scrubbed (leave skin on)
4–5 eggs
4–5 cups finely shredded savoy
  cabbage
4–5 handfuls mung bean sprouts
1 telegraph cucumber, thinly sliced
1 bunch radishes, thinly sliced
1 red, yellow or orange capsicum,
  core and seeds removed,
  thinly sliced

SATAY SAUCE

2 cloves garlic, minced
1 red onion, finely diced
1 stalk lemongrass, tough outer skin
  removed and finely chopped
1 red chilli, finely sliced
2 teaspoons fish sauce
2 tablespoons soy sauce
1 cup finely chopped roasted peanuts
1 x 400g can coconut milk
2 teaspoons brown sugar
2 teaspoons lemon or lime juice

TO SERVE

¼ cup chopped roasted peanuts
½ cup chopped coriander and
  mint leaves
½ red chilli, thinly sliced (optional)
1 lime, cut into wedges

1 Place tofu and marinade ingredients in a shallow dish and leave to marinate while you prepare rest of meal. Alternatively, marinate overnight.

2 Cut any larger potatoes in half, so they are all roughly the same size. Place in a pot with 1 teaspoon salt, cover with water and bring to the boil. Cook for about 8–10 minutes, then use a spoon to gently add whole eggs to pot and simmer for a further 5 minutes. Drain and run eggs under cold water to help stop the cooking process. Carefully peel eggs and set aside.

3 While potatoes and eggs cook, make the satay sauce. Heat a drizzle of oil in a small pot on medium heat. Cook garlic, onion, lemongrass and chilli until fragrant and golden, about 2 minutes. Add remaining satay sauce ingredients (except lemon or lime juice) and simmer for about 10 minutes until thickened. Add lemon or lime juice and season with extra brown sugar, if desired. Keep warm.

4 Heat a drizzle of oil in a large fry-pan (preferably non-stick) on medium heat. Cook tofu for 1–2 minutes each side, until golden. Remove from pan and set aside. Add cabbage and stir-fry for about 2 minutes until wilted. Set aside.

TO SERVE divide potatoes, cabbage and remaining salad ingredients between plates. Cut eggs in half and place on top of salad, along with a few slices of tofu. Spoon over satay sauce and sprinkle with peanuts, herbs and chilli (if using). Squeeze over lime juice just before eating.

ENERGY	2658kJ (633kcal)
CARBOHYDRATE	41.5g
PROTEIN	31.5g
FAT	36.8g

   omit fish sauce use GF soy sauce

MY SWEET **SUMMER** RECIPES

TANDOORI CHARRED FISH AND CHIPS WITH SALAD

SERVES 4–5
READY IN: 40 MINUTES
PREP TIME: 15 MINUTES
COOK TIME: 25–30 MINUTES

CHIPS
800g agria potatoes, scrubbed
   (leave skin on)
1 tablespoon olive oil

TANDOORI CHARRED FISH
600g boneless, skinless white
   fish fillets
2 tablespoons tandoori paste
   (store-bought or see page 179)
1 tablespoon olive oil

SALAD
½ small red onion, thinly sliced
3 carrots, peeled and cut into thin
   matchsticks or coarsely grated
1 red capsicum, core and seeds
   removed, thinly sliced
½ cos or iceberg lettuce, finely
   sliced
¼ cup finely chopped coriander
   leaves
¼ cup finely chopped mint leaves
¼ cup golden raisins or sultanas
¼ cup sliced almonds
juice of ½ lemon

GARLIC YOGHURT
½ cup natural unsweetened
   yoghurt
1 small clove garlic, minced
zest and juice of ½ lemon

TO SERVE
1 lemon, cut into wedges

PREHEAT oven to 220°C. Line an oven tray with baking paper.

1 Cut potatoes into 1cm thick slices then into 1cm chips. Toss with olive oil in prepared tray and season with salt and pepper. Bake for 25–30 minutes until golden and crispy. Turn once during cooking.

2 Pat fish dry with paper towels and remove any remaining scales or bones. Rub tandoori paste all over fish. Set aside to marinate at room temperature while you prepare the salad.

3 Place salad ingredients in a large serving bowl and toss with a drizzle of extra virgin olive oil to combine. In a small bowl mix all garlic yoghurt ingredients together. Set aside.

4 Heat oil in a large fry-pan (preferably non-stick) on medium heat. Season fish with salt and cook, in batches, for 1–2 minutes each side until just cooked through.

TO SERVE place some chips, salad and a piece of tandoori charred fish on each plate and drizzle over garlic yoghurt and a squeeze of lemon.

ENERGY	1999kJ (476kcal)
CARBOHYDRATE	41.0g
PROTEIN	32.1g
FAT	219.5g

   omit yoghurt

> "This blew me away. The carrot and raisin salad was amazing."

KIRA

BEEF SCOTCH FILLET WITH CHERRY TOMATOES, ASPARAGUS, BEANS AND CHIMICHURRI

SERVES 4–5
READY IN: 25 MINUTES
PREP TIME: 10 MINUTES
COOK TIME: 15 MINUTES

BEEF AND GREENS

600g beef scotch fillet (at room temperature)
200g green beans, trimmed
1 bunch asparagus (about 12 spears), trimmed

CHERRY TOMATOES AND BEANS

2 punnets cherry tomatoes
2 x 400g cans cannellini beans, drained and rinsed

TO SERVE

½ cup chimichurri (see page 176)

PREHEAT BBQ grill to high (if using).

1 Start by making the chimichurri (see page 176).

2 Pat beef dry with paper towels and season with salt. Heat a drizzle of oil in a large fry-pan on high heat and cook beef for about 2 minutes each side for medium-rare (depending on thickness) or until cooked to your liking. Alternatively cook on BBQ. Set aside on a plate, covered with foil, to rest for 5–10 minutes while you prepare rest of meal. Keep pan on heat.

3 In same pan, cook green beans for 3 minutes, until bright green and just tender. Add 1–2 tablespoons water to create steam and cook beans through. Set aside with steak. Keep pan on heat. Add asparagus to pan and a little more water and cook for 1–2 minutes until tender. Remove from pan and set aside with green beans.

4 Add cherry tomatoes to pan and cook for 1–2 minutes until starting to soften and blister. Add cannellini beans and toss with tomatoes to just warm through. Turn off heat, gently toss through 2 tablespoons chimichurri and season to taste with salt and pepper. Slice beef against the grain.

TO SERVE spoon some cherry tomatoes and beans onto each plate and top with green beans, asparagus and beef. Drizzle over remaining chimichurri.

ENERGY	1890kJ (450kcal)
CARBOHYDRATE	27.0g
PROTEIN	40.1g
FAT	18.6g

LESS TIME   DAIRY FREE   GLUTEN FREE   BBQ

LEMON AND CHILLI CURED SALMON WITH HORSERADISH POTATO SALAD AND ASPARAGUS

SERVES 4–5
READY IN: 35 MINUTES
PREP TIME: 20 MINUTES
COOK TIME: 15 MINUTES

HORSERADISH POTATO SALAD

700–800g waxy baby potatoes, scrubbed and diced 2cm (leave skin on)
juice of 2 lemons (reserve zest for salmon)
¼ cup chopped parsley
3–4 tablespoons horseradish sauce (store-bought)
¼ cup mayonnaise
3 spring onions, thinly sliced

LEMON AND CHILLI CURED SALMON

600g skinless salmon fillet, cut into 4–5 fillets
½ –1 red chilli, finely chopped (seeds removed for less heat)
zest of 2 lemons
1 teaspoon sugar
1 teaspoon salt

ASPARAGUS

2 bunches asparagus (about 24 spears), trimmed

TO SERVE

1 spring onion, thinly sliced on an angle
½ cup torn flat-leaf parsley leaves
1 lemon, cut into wedges

PREHEAT oven to 220°C. Bring a large pot of salted water to the boil. Line an oven tray with baking paper.

1 Cook potatoes in pot of boiling water for about 10 minutes or until just tender. Drain, transfer to a large plate and place in refrigerator to cool until needed.

2 Pat salmon dry with paper towels and remove any pin bones. In a small bowl mix chilli, lemon zest, sugar and salt together. Sprinkle over salmon and gently press down, then set aside to cure for 3–4 minutes.

3 Place salmon on prepared tray and bake for 5–7 minutes (depending on thickness), or until salmon is cooked medium. Remove from oven to rest for a few minutes.

4 Bring a large pot of salted water to the boil and cook asparagus for 1–2 minutes until bright green and tender, then drain. Season with salt and pepper and toss with a drizzle of olive oil.

5 In a medium bowl combine lemon juice, parsley, horseradish sauce, mayonnaise and spring onions. Add potatoes and toss to coat. Season to taste with salt and pepper.

TO SERVE divide horseradish potato salad between plates with asparagus on the side. Top with cured salmon and sprinkle over spring onion and parsley. Squeeze over lemon juice just before eating.

ENERGY	2690kJ (640kcal)
CARBOHYDRATE	32.0g
PROTEIN	31.1g
FAT	43.0g

"
This was absolutely scrumptious. The corn salsa and chicken stuffing was divine."

SARAH

CHICKEN WITH PISTACHIO THYME STUFFING AND GRILLED CORN SALSA

SERVES 4–5
READY IN: 40 MINUTES
PREP TIME: 20 MINUTES
COOK TIME: 25 MINUTES

CHICKEN WITH PISTACHIO THYME STUFFING

¼ cup pistachio nuts
3–4 tablespoons finely chopped
  thyme leaves
1 tablespoon olive oil
1 tablespoon runny honey
80g thinly sliced prosciutto
600g boneless, skinless chicken
  thighs

GRILLED CORN SALSA

4 corncobs, husk and silk removed
1 red chilli, seeds removed, finely
  sliced
1 tablespoon olive oil
¼ cup finely sliced chives
zest and juice of 1 lime

SALAD

4–5 handfuls rocket or salad
  leaves
1 bunch (4–5) baby radishes,
  trimmed and thinly sliced
2 tablespoons poppy seeds
  (optional)
1 tablespoon extra virgin olive oil
juice of 1 lime

TO SERVE

1 lime, cut into wedges (optional)

PREHEAT oven to 200°C. Line an oven tray with baking paper.

1 Finely chop pistachios (or blitz in a food processor) and combine with thyme, olive oil and honey.

2 Lay one prosciutto slice (with the short end facing you) on prepared tray. Lay one of the chicken thighs on top (tuck under overhanging flesh) and sprinkle pistachio mixture over chicken (about 1–2 teaspoons per thigh). Roll prosciutto and chicken over on themselves, so they are tightly wrapped. Repeat with remaining prosciutto and chicken thighs. Place on prepared tray and bake for 15–18 minutes or until cooked through.

3 While chicken cooks, prepare rest of meal. Remove corn kernels from cobs, by first slicing one end off the cob so it can stand up straight without wobbling, then use a sharp knife to slice downwards. Combine with chilli and olive oil in a small bowl and set aside. Toss all salad ingredients together.

4 When chicken is cooked, change oven setting to grill, scatter corn and chilli around chicken and place on a higher rack in the oven (not at the very top or it may burn). Grill until prosciutto is brown and crispy, 3–5 minutes. Remove chicken from oven and set aside to rest for a few minutes. Return corn to oven to continue grilling for 1–2 minutes until slightly golden. Toss corn and chilli with chives and lime zest and juice.

TO SERVE place a handful of salad, some grilled corn salsa and 1–2 chicken thighs on each plate. Squeeze over extra lime juice just before eating, if desired.

ENERGY	1972kJ (470kcal)
CARBOHYDRATE	27.2g
PROTEIN	38.0g
FAT	22.3g

 MED TIME DAIRY FREE GLUTEN FREE

GRILLED CHICKEN AND VEGETABLE STACKS WITH CREAMY FETA

SERVES 4–5
READY IN: 40 MINUTES
PREP TIME: 20 MINUTES
COOK TIME: 25 MINUTES

GRILLED CHICKEN

600g boneless, skinless chicken
  breasts
1 tablespoon olive oil
zest and juice of 1 lemon
2 cloves garlic, minced
2–3 tablespoons finely chopped
  thyme leaves

VEGETABLES

800g golden or orange kumara,
  scrubbed (leave skin on) and
  sliced into 1cm thick rounds
2 red capsicums, core and seeds
  removed, quartered
2 courgettes, trimmed and sliced
  lengthways 1cm thick
1 eggplant, trimmed and sliced
  lengthways 1cm thick

CREAMY FETA

70g feta cheese, crumbled
½ cup natural unsweetened
  yoghurt
¼ cup finely chopped mint leaves

TO SERVE

150g baby spinach leaves
¼ cup mint leaves

PREHEAT oven to 200°C. Line two oven trays with baking paper. Preheat BBQ grill to medium to high heat (if using).

1 Pat chicken dry with paper towels and cut into steaks. To do this, place one hand flat on top of chicken breast and use a knife to slice through horizontally to make 2 thin steaks, trying to keep equal thickness on each side. Combine with olive oil, lemon zest and juice, garlic and thyme and set aside to marinate at room temperature.

2 Toss kumara and capsicum with a drizzle of olive oil in first prepared tray and arrange in a single layer. Season with salt and pepper and roast for 20–25 minutes until kumara is golden and tender. Turn once during cooking. Toss courgettes and eggplant with another drizzle of olive oil in other prepared tray (you may need to overlap courgettes and eggplant slightly so they all fit). Season with salt and pepper and roast for about 20 minutes until soft and eggplant is lightly browned. Alternatively, cook vegetables on BBQ grill.

3 Heat a drizzle of oil in a large fry-pan (or use BBQ grill) on medium to high heat. Season chicken with salt and cook, in batches, for 2–3 minutes each side or until golden and cooked through. Set aside to rest for a few minutes.

4 In a small bowl combine feta, yoghurt and mint and mix with a fork until smooth.

TO SERVE layer kumara, vegetables, spinach, chicken and creamy feta on each plate. Spoon over extra creamy feta and garnish with mint.

ENERGY	1878kJ (447kcal)
CARBOHYDRATE	42.7g
PROTEIN	39.0g
FAT	12.1g

    omit feta and yoghurt

"
My kind of dish!
Loved all the veges.
The chicken was a hit
with the whole family."

MICHELLE

> "Huge hit with the kids — the Mexican spices were delicious and a wonderful accompaniment to the fish."

HELEN

FISH BURGERS WITH TOMATO AVOCADO SALSA AND MEXICAN WEDGES

SERVES 4–5
READY IN: 45 MINUTES
PREP TIME: 20 MINUTES
COOK TIME: 30 MINUTES

MEXICAN WEDGES

500g agria potatoes, scrubbed
  (leave skin on)
2 teaspoons Mexican spice mix
  (see page 177)

TOMATO AVOCADO SALSA

2 tomatoes, diced
¼ red onion, finely diced
flesh of 1 avocado, diced
1 yellow capsicum, core and seeds
  removed, finely diced
2 tablespoons chopped coriander
  leaves
juice of ½ lemon or lime

FISH

3 tablespoons flour
½ teaspoon salt
¼ teaspoon freshly ground
  black pepper
600g boneless, skinless white
  fish fillets

TO SERVE

3–4 tablespoons mayonnaise
½ teaspoon Mexican spice mix
  (see page 177)
juice of ½ lemon or lime
½ iceberg lettuce, shredded
4–5 burger buns, cut in half
  horizontally
2–3 tablespoons tomato chutney,
  tomato sauce or chipotle sauce

PREHEAT oven to 200°C. Line an oven tray with baking paper.

1 Cut potatoes in half lengthways then into 1.5cm thick wedges. Toss with Mexican spice mix and a drizzle of olive oil in prepared tray. Season well with salt and roast for about 30 minutes until golden and crisp. Turn once during cooking.

2 Combine all tomato avocado salsa ingredients in a medium bowl. Season to taste with salt and pepper. Set aside.

3 On a shallow plate or dish combine flour, salt and pepper. Pat fish dry with paper towels and remove any remaining scales or bones. Cut fillets to roughly fit burger buns and coat in seasoned flour, shaking off excess. Heat a drizzle of oil in a large fry-pan on medium heat. Cook fish, in batches, for 1–2 minutes each side until lightly golden and just cooked through.

4 Combine mayonnaise with Mexican spice mix and lemon or lime juice. Toss shredded lettuce with half of the mayo mixture (reserve remainder for serving) and set aside. Place burger buns in the oven for 2–3 minutes until warmed through.

TO SERVE spread a little Mexican mayo over one half of each burger bun, and tomato chutney or sauce over the other half. Fill with a piece of fish, some lettuce and tomato avocado salsa. Serve with Mexican wedges on the side.

ENERGY	2664kJ (634kcal)
CARBOHYDRATE	65.3g
PROTEIN	37.3g
FAT	23.4g

MED TIME   DAIRY FREE

PORK STEAKS WITH KUMARA ROSTI, NECTARINE SALSA AND CURRY MAYO

SERVES 4–5
READY IN: 35 MINUTES
PREP TIME: 20 MINUTES
COOK TIME: 15 MINUTES

KUMARA ROSTI

800g orange or golden kumara,
peeled then grated until you
have 4–5 cups
2 eggs
¾ teaspoon salt
½ teaspoon freshly ground
black pepper
¼ cup cornflour
2 tablespoons oil

PORK STEAKS

600g pork sirloin steaks (at room
temperature)
1 teaspoon mild curry powder

NECTARINE SALSA

2 nectarines, diced
½ red onion, peeled and
finely diced
2 tomatoes, diced
1 carrot, peeled and cut into thin
matchsticks or grated
1 Lebanese cucumber, quartered
lengthways, diced
juice of ½ lime or lemon
¼ cup chopped coriander leaves

CURRY MAYO

¼ cup mayonnaise
1 teaspoon mild curry powder
juice of ½ lime or lemon

TO SERVE

a few coriander leaves
1 lime or lemon, cut into wedges

PREHEAT BBQ grill to medium to high (if using).

1 Combine grated kumara with eggs, salt, pepper and cornflour in a large bowl and mix well. Use a one-third cup measure to scoop out mixture and roll into balls. Heat oil in a large, non-stick fry-pan on medium heat. Place kumara balls in the hot pan and flatten with a fish slice to make rosti about 1cm thick. Cook, in batches, for 2–3 minutes on one side until a golden crust has formed, then flip over and cook the other side for 2–3 minutes. Add a little more oil as needed.

2 Pat pork dry with paper towels, dust with curry powder and season with salt. Heat a drizzle of oil in a separate large fry-pan on medium to high heat and cook pork for about 3 minutes each side or until just cooked through (depending on thickness). Alternatively, cook on BBQ. Set aside, covered with foil, to rest for 5 minutes before slicing thinly.

3 Mix all nectarine salsa ingredients together with a drizzle of extra virgin olive oil and season to taste with a little salt and pepper. In a small bowl mix all curry mayo ingredients together.

TO SERVE divide kumara rosti among plates and top with slices of pork and some nectarine salsa. Serve with a dollop of curry mayo on the side. Garnish with coriander and squeeze over lime or lemon juice just before serving.

ENERGY	2637kJ (628kcal)
CARBOHYDRATE	48.6g
PROTEIN	32.5g
FAT	33.4g

 MED TIME DAIRY FREE GLUTEN FREE BBQ

"
Loved it all. Salsa
was fresh and
light and perfect
for a hot summer
night's dinner."

LISA

"

Delicious recipe. So
easy to make and looked
incredible (after all, we do
eat with our eyes first!).
It tasted amazing as well!"

LEILA

OPEN LASAGNE OF COURGETTES, ARTICHOKES, GOAT'S CHEESE AND PESTO

SERVES 5
READY IN: 30 MINUTES
PREP TIME: 15 MINUTES
COOK TIME: 15 MINUTES

OPEN LASAGNE

1 tablespoon olive oil
2 shallots, finely diced
1 cup white wine
2 courgettes, trimmed and sliced
  0.5cm
1 bunch asparagus (about 12
  spears), trimmed and sliced into
  4cm lengths
½ red chilli, finely chopped
  (optional)
200g marinated artichokes (from
  a jar), drained and roughly
  chopped
½ cup water
150g soft goat's cheese
6 tablespoons basil pesto
  (store-bought or see page 178)
200g baby spinach leaves
400g fresh pasta sheets

TO SERVE

2 tablespoons basil pesto
  (store-bought or see page 178)
50g soft goat's cheese
¼ cup sliced basil leaves
½ cup chopped toasted walnuts*

BRING a large pot of salted water to the boil.

1 Heat oil in a large fry-pan on medium heat. Cook shallots for 4–5 minutes until soft. Add wine, increase heat and bring to the boil. Boil for 4–5 minutes until all liquid has evaporated. Add courgettes, asparagus and chilli (if using) and stir-fry for about 2 minutes. Stir through artichokes and water, stir to combine and cook for a further minute. Turn off heat, break goat's cheese into pan and stir through pesto and spinach. Season to taste with salt and freshly ground black pepper.

2 Cut pasta sheets into roughly 8cm squares. Separate sheets and cook in pot of boiling water for about 3 minutes or until al dente (just tender). Drain pasta then toss with a drizzle of extra virgin olive oil.

TO SERVE place 1 pasta sheet in each serving bowl or plate and top with some vegetable mixture, dividing equally. Place another pasta sheet on top with more vegetable mixture and repeat until you have used 3–4 pasta sheets per serving. Drizzle over a little pesto and crumble over goat's cheese. Garnish with basil leaves and walnuts.

*TIP

Toast walnuts in a small, dry fry-pan on medium heat for 1–2 minutes until light golden, moving pan frequently to avoid burning. Remove from pan and roughly chop.

ENERGY	2727kJ (649kcal)
CARBOHYDRATE	51.8g
PROTEIN	23.0g
FAT	33.8g

SPICED CHICKEN AND MANGO PIZZAS WITH CURRY MAYO

SERVES 4–5
READY IN: 35 MINUTES
PREP TIME: 15 MINUTES
COOK TIME: 20 MINUTES

SPICED CHICKEN AND MANGO PIZZAS

400g boneless, skinless chicken
   breasts or thighs
1 teaspoon paprika
1 teaspoon mild curry powder
½ teaspoon turmeric
½ teaspoon garam masala
¼ teaspoon salt
6 tablespoons tomato paste
1 tablespoon olive oil
1 red onion, peeled and
   thinly sliced
2 large (or 3 medium) pizza bases
   (store-bought or see page 180)
2 cups grated mozzarella cheese
1 mango, peeled and thinly sliced
2 green capsicums, core and
   seeds removed, thinly sliced

CURRY MAYO

3 tablespoons mayonnaise
½ teaspoon curry powder
2 teaspoons sweet chilli sauce
1 teaspoon white wine vinegar

TO SERVE

150g baby spinach leaves

PREHEAT oven to 220°C. Preheat three oven trays (or pizza stones).

1 Pat chicken dry with paper towels and cut into 1cm strips. Place in a medium dish with spices and salt, mix well then marinate for 5 minutes while you prepare rest of meal. In a small bowl mix tomato paste with olive oil and set aside.

2 Heat a drizzle of oil in a medium fry-pan on medium to high heat. Fry onion for 3 minutes until softened and golden. Remove from pan and set aside. Add a drizzle more oil to the pan and fry chicken for about 1 minute each side until golden (but not completely cooked through).

3 Lay 3 sheets of baking paper on the bench and place a pizza base on top of each. Divide tomato paste and oil mixture between bases and spread to cover. Sprinkle cheese evenly over bases, then top with onion, chicken, mango and capsicum.

4 Carefully lift up the baking paper with the pizzas on top and place on preheated trays then carefully slide baking paper away (use a fish slice to help with this). Cook pizzas until the bases are crisp and golden around the edges, 12–14 minutes. Swap position of trays halfway through cooking time so they cook evenly.

5 While pizza is cooking, mix all curry mayo ingredients together in a bowl and set aside.

TO SERVE cut pizzas into wedges, place a few pieces onto plates with spinach leaves scattered over. Drizzle curry mayo over spinach and pizzas.

ENERGY	2486kJ (592kcal)
CARBOHYDRATE	51.6g
PROTEIN	40.3g
FAT	24.2g

 Nutrition based on two large pizza bases

SUMAC LAMB AND EGGPLANT KEBABS WITH MINT YOGHURT

SERVES 4–5
READY IN: 30 MINUTES
PREP TIME: 15 MINUTES
COOK TIME: 15 MINUTES

LAMB AND EGGPLANT KEBABS
2 tablespoons olive oil
2 eggplants, sliced into 1.5cm
   rounds
1 tablespoon sumac (optional)
600g lamb rump steaks (at room
   temperature)

MINT YOGHURT
1 cup natural unsweetened yoghurt
¼ cup chopped mint leaves
1–2 teaspoons runny honey
1 clove garlic, minced

TO SERVE
4–5 flat breads or wraps
   (store-bought)
½ red onion, thinly sliced
1 iceberg or cos lettuce (or any
   salad greens), finely shredded
2 carrots, peeled and cut into thin
   matchsticks or grated
¼ cup chopped parsley
2 tomatoes, thinly sliced
2 teaspoons sumac (optional)
¼ cup sliced mint leaves

PREHEAT BBQ grill to medium to high (if using).

1 Heat olive oil in a large fry-pan on medium heat (or use BBQ grill). Season eggplant with salt and fry, in batches, for about 2 minutes each side until golden. Remove from pan, sprinkle with sumac (if using) and set aside.

2 Pat lamb dry with paper towels and season with salt and pepper. Increase heat to high (or use BBQ grill), add a drizzle of olive oil and fry lamb for 2–3 minutes each side for medium-rare (depending on thickness) or until cooked to your liking. Remove from heat, cover and rest for 3 minutes.

3 In a small bowl mix all mint yoghurt ingredients together well and season with salt and pepper.

4 In same pan lamb was cooked in, reduce heat to medium (or use BBQ grill) and toast flat breads or wraps for 30 seconds each side until softened. Alternatively, wrap stack of flat breads or wraps in foil and warm in pan or on BBQ for 2–3 minutes. Slice lamb thinly against the grain.

TO SERVE fill flat breads or wraps with onion, lettuce, carrot, parsley, tomatoes, eggplant slices and some lamb. Finish with a dollop of mint yoghurt, a sprinkle of sumac (if using) and mint leaves. Roll up and enjoy!

ENERGY	2357kJ (561kcal)
CARBOHYDRATE	49.3g
PROTEIN	40.8g
FAT	19.4g

   omit yoghurt

PAN-FRIED FISH AND NOODLE SALAD WITH WASABI GINGER SOY DRESSING

SERVES 4–5
READY IN: 25 MINUTES
PREP TIME: 15 MINUTES
COOK TIME: 10 MINUTES

PAN-FRIED FISH AND NOODLE SALAD

200g dried mung bean vermicelli
  (glass noodles)
1 mango, peeled and thinly sliced
2 carrots, peeled and cut into thin
  matchsticks or grated
2 red capsicums, core and seeds
  removed, cut into thin strips
4 spring onions, finely sliced on
  an angle
600g boneless, skinless white
  fish fillets

WASABI GINGER SOY DRESSING

3–4 teaspoons finely grated
  ginger
2 tablespoons extra virgin olive oil
2 tablespoons soy sauce
3–4 tablespoons rice vinegar
2 teaspoons wasabi paste
2 teaspoons runny honey

TO SERVE

2 tablespoons toasted sesame
  seeds*
1 lime, cut into wedges
¼ cup coriander leaves

BRING a full kettle to the boil.

1 Place vermicelli in a large, heat-proof bowl and pour boiling water over to cover. Use a fork and mix well to separate strands, then cover and leave to soak for about 4 minutes until soft. Drain, rinse under cold water and drain well again. Snip noodles in a few places with scissors, to shorten noodle strands.

2 Place mango and vegetables in a large bowl with the drained vermicelli.

3 Whisk all dressing ingredients together in a small bowl. Pour half over salad and toss to combine.

4 Pat fish dry with paper towels, removing any remaining scales or bones, and season with salt. Heat a drizzle of oil in a large fry-pan on high heat. Cook fish for 1–2 minutes each side until just cooked through.

TO SERVE divide noodle salad between plates and top with a piece of fish. Drizzle over remaining wasabi ginger soy dressing and sprinkle with toasted sesame seeds. Serve with a wedge of lime to squeeze over and garnish with some coriander leaves.

*TIP

Toast sesame seeds in a small, dry fry-pan on medium heat for 30–60 seconds until light golden, moving pan frequently to avoid burning.

ENERGY	1733kJ (413kcal)
CARBOHYDRATE	52.4g
PROTEIN	26.5g
FAT	10.2g

   use GF soy sauce

"
Loved this recipe. The Thai chicken cakes were fabulous and the quinoa salad was a perfect accompaniment."

SYLVIA

THAI CHICKEN CAKES WITH MANGO, COURGETTE AND QUINOA SALAD

SERVES 4–5
READY IN: 35 MINUTES
PREP TIME: 20 MINUTES
COOK TIME: 25 MINUTES

THAI CHICKEN CAKES

600g chicken mince
6 tablespoons panko
 breadcrumbs
2 teaspoons store-bought Thai
 red or green curry paste or
 4 teaspoons homemade Thai
 red or green curry paste
 (see page 178)
2 tablespoons lemon or lime juice
4 teaspoons fish sauce
2 cloves garlic, minced
2 teaspoons finely grated ginger
100g green beans, trimmed and
 very finely sliced
1 tablespoon oil

MANGO, COURGETTE AND QUINOA SALAD

1½ cups water
1 cup quinoa
½ teaspoon salt
2 courgettes
4 spring onions, finely sliced
1 mango, peeled and
 roughly diced

DRESSING

2 tablespoons extra virgin olive oil
4 teaspoons soy sauce
¼ cup rice vinegar
2 teaspoons fish sauce
2 teaspoons runny honey

TO SERVE

½ cup coriander leaves

PREHEAT oven to 200°C. Line an oven tray with baking paper.

1 In a large bowl mix together all Thai chicken cake ingredients (except oil) with clean hands. Use a quarter cup measure to scoop mixture out and shape into patties. Place on a plate and refrigerate while you prepare quinoa salad.

2 Bring water to the boil in a medium pot on high heat. As soon as it boils, add quinoa and salt. Cover with a tight-fitting lid and reduce to low heat to cook for 12 minutes. Turn off heat and leave to steam, still covered, for a further 8 minutes. Do not lift lid at any time during cooking.

3 While quinoa is cooking prepare rest of meal. Mix all dressing ingredients together in a small bowl. Use a vegetable peeler to peel courgettes into long ribbons (stopping when you get to the core). Finely slice the core. Place vegetables and mango in a large bowl.

4 Heat oil in a large fry-pan (preferably non-stick) on medium to high heat. Fry chicken cakes for about 2 minutes each side, until golden, pushing down on them slightly with a fish slice to help create a crust (they don't need to be fully cooked yet). Transfer to prepared tray and bake for a further 7–9 minutes or until cooked through. Transfer to a plate lined with paper towels and rest, covered, for 2–3 minutes.

5 Add cooked quinoa and dressing to bowl with vegetables and mango. Toss to combine.

TO SERVE divide mango, courgette and quinoa salad between bowls and top with a few Thai chicken cakes. Garnish with coriander.

ENERGY	2027kJ (483kcal)
CARBOHYDRATE	38.9g
PROTEIN	33.9g
FAT	21.0g

   use GF soy sauce
and breadcrumbs

VENISON WITH CRUMBED EGGPLANT, GREENS AND RED WINE CHERRIES

SERVES 4–5
READY IN: 45 MINUTES
PREP TIME: 25 MINUTES
COOK TIME: 20 MINUTES

RED WINE CHERRIES

½ cup red wine
2 tablespoons white vinegar
2 tablespoons soy sauce
1 teaspoon sesame oil
4 teaspoons sugar
1 red chilli, seeds removed and finely chopped
200g cherries, halved and stones removed (scoop out with a teaspoon)
2 tablespoons finely sliced chives

CRUMBED EGGPLANT AND VENISON

½ cup flour
1 teaspoon salt
2 eggs
½ cup milk
1½ cups panko breadcrumbs
1 eggplant, sliced into 0.5cm thick rounds
2 tablespoons olive oil
600g venison medallions (at room temperature)
300g green beans, trimmed
2 bunches asparagus (about 24 spears), trimmed

TO SERVE

2 tablespoons toasted sesame seeds*

PREHEAT BBQ grill to high (if using).

1 In a small pot, bring red wine, vinegar, soy sauce, sesame oil, sugar and chilli to the boil. Simmer for 3–4 minutes until reduced by half, then remove from heat and add cherries. Set aside to cool.

2 Combine flour and salt in one bowl, whisk eggs and milk in a second bowl and place panko breadcrumbs in a third bowl. Coat eggplant slices first in flour, then egg mixture and finally breadcrumbs, shaking off excess as you go. Heat oil in a large fry-pan on medium heat. Cook eggplant in batches for about 2 minutes each side until golden brown and cooked through. Add extra oil if needed. Set aside on paper towels.

3 Keep pan on heat and increase temperature to high (or use BBQ grill). Pat venison dry with paper towels and season with salt. Cook for about 2 minutes each side for medium-rare (depending on thickness), or until cooked to your liking. Transfer to a plate to rest, covered with foil, for 5–10 minutes.

4 Bring a large pot of salted water to the boil. Cook beans and asparagus for 2–3 minutes, then drain. Stir chives through cherries and slice venison against the grain.

TO SERVE place a few crumbed eggplant slices on each plate. Arrange venison on top and greens to the side. Spoon over some red wine cherries and drizzle over sauce. Sprinkle with sesame seeds.

*TIP

Toast sesame seeds in a small, dry fry-pan on medium heat for 30–60 seconds until light golden, moving pan frequently to avoid burning.

ENERGY	2198kJ (523kcal)
CARBOHYDRATE	42.6g
PROTEIN	44.5g
FAT	15.8g

   use GF breadcrumbs, flour and soy sauce

"
I love eggplant but am
never quite sure what to do
with it. The cherry sauce
was divine. Wonderful."

CHRIS

"
Everyone loved this one.
A spectacular success!"
MORAG

CHICKEN KATSU WITH CORN AND BOK CHOY BROWN RICE SALAD

SERVES 4—5
READY IN: 40 MINUTES
PREP TIME: 20 MINUTES
COOK TIME: 35 MINUTES

CHICKEN KATSU

600g boneless, skinless chicken
    breasts
¼ cup flour
½ teaspoon salt
2 eggs
1½ cups panko breadcrumbs
2 tablespoons oil

BROWN RICE SALAD

3 cups steamed brown rice (see
    page 176)
2 corncobs, husk and silk removed
2—3 baby bok choy, bottom 3cm
    trimmed, washed and finely
    sliced
1 red, orange or yellow capsicum,
    core and seeds removed, sliced
¼ cup chopped coriander leaves
⅓ cup chopped roasted peanuts

DRESSING

1½ tablespoons soy sauce
2 tablespoons lemon juice
1 teaspoon sesame oil
1 tablespoon sweet chilli sauce
½ clove garlic, minced
1.5cm piece ginger, finely grated

TO SERVE

¼—½ cup katsu sauce (store-
    bought or see page 178)
a few coriander leaves

PREHEAT oven to 200°C. Bring a full kettle to the boil. Line an oven tray with baking paper.

1 Start by cooking the brown rice for the salad. While rice is cooking, prepare rest of meal. Pat chicken dry with paper towels and cut into steaks. To do this, place one hand flat on top of each chicken breast and use a knife to slice through horizontally to make 2 thin steaks, trying to keep equal thickness on each side.

2 Mix flour with salt in one dish, whisk eggs in a second dish and place panko breadcrumbs in a third dish. Coat each chicken steak first in flour, then eggs, then panko breadcrumbs. Set aside on a clean, dry plate.

3 Place corncobs in a dish, cover with boiling water and leave for 2—3 minutes. Drain corn and cut off kernels, by first slicing one end off the cob so it can stand up straight without wobbling, then use a sharp knife to slice downwards. In a large bowl, toss corn, bok choy, capsicum and coriander with peanuts.

4 Heat oil in a large fry-pan (preferably non-stick) on medium heat. Fry chicken, in batches, for 1—2 minutes each side until golden brown. Transfer to prepared tray and bake for about 5 minutes to finish cooking through. Slice chicken to serve, if desired.

5 Mix all dressing ingredients together well and toss with brown rice and vegetables just before serving.

TO SERVE spoon some brown rice salad onto each plate, with some crumbed chicken. Drizzle over katsu sauce and garnish with coriander.

ENERGY	2915kJ (694kcal)
CARBOHYDRATE	78.1g
PROTEIN	47.8g
FAT	21.0g

VENISON IN LETTUCE CUPS WITH KUMARA WEDGES AND TOMATO BASIL SALSA

SERVES 4–5
READY IN: 40 MINUTES
PREP TIME: 20 MINUTES
COOK TIME: 30 MINUTES

VENISON PATTIES
½ cup panko breadcrumbs
¼ cup milk
600g venison mince
¾ red onion, finely diced
   (reserve remaining ¼ for salsa)
¼ cup chopped parsley leaves
   and stalks
¾ teaspoon salt
¼ teaspoon freshly ground
   black pepper
1 courgette, grated

KUMARA WEDGES
800g mixed kumara, scrubbed
   (leave skin on) and cut into
   1–2cm thick wedges
1 tablespoon olive oil

TOMATO BASIL SALSA
2 tomatoes, diced 1cm
¼ cup roughly chopped
   basil leaves
¼ red onion, finely diced
1 tablespoon extra virgin olive oil

TO SERVE
1 baby cos lettuce, leaves
   separated
100g feta cheese, crumbled

PREHEAT oven to 200°C. Line an oven tray with baking paper. Preheat BBQ hot plate to medium (if using).

1 In a large bowl, soak panko breadcrumbs with milk for a few minutes.

2 Toss kumara with oil on prepared tray. Season with salt and bake for 20–30 minutes until golden and tender. Turn once during cooking.

3 Add all remaining venison patty ingredients to the bowl with breadcrumbs and milk. Use clean hands to mix thoroughly. Use a ¼ cup measure to scoop out mixture and shape into patties. Place on a plate and refrigerate for 5 minutes to firm up a little while you prepare salsa.

4 Mix all tomato basil salsa ingredients together in a small bowl. Season with salt and pepper and set aside.

5 Heat a drizzle of oil in a large fry-pan (preferably non-stick) on medium heat (or use BBQ hot plate). Fry venison patties for about 4 minutes on one side then turn over and press down with a fish slice. Fry for a further 4 minutes until just cooked through. Rest on a plate, covered, for 2 minutes.

TO SERVE divide kumara wedges between plates. To assemble, place a venison patty into a lettuce leaf, spoon over tomato basil salsa and crumble over a little feta cheese.

ENERGY	2181kJ (519kcal)
CARBOHYDRATE	54.8g
PROTEIN	36.6g
FAT	15.9g

   use dairy free milk, omit feta use GF breadcrumbs

> " Great flavours
> and awesome
> alternative to buns.
> Will definitely
> repeat this!"
>
> **TAMRYN**

"Family LOVED this one! They voted it best pizza EVER!"

JANE

SMOKED SALMON PIZZAS WITH LEMON SOUR CREAM, CAPERS, AND COURGETTE CRANBERRY SALAD

SERVES 4–5
READY IN: 30 MINUTES
PREP TIME: 20 MINUTES
COOK TIME: 15 MINUTES

PIZZAS

1 x 400g can crushed tomatoes
1 clove garlic, minced
1 tablespoon olive oil
2 large pizza bases (store-bought or see page 180)
½ red onion, finely diced
1 punnet cherry tomatoes, cut in half
1–1½ cups grated mozzarella cheese
200g hot smoked salmon
1–2 tablespoons chopped capers (optional)

COURGETTE CRANBERRY SALAD

3 courgettes
¼ cup finely chopped parsley
¼ cup roughly chopped dried cranberries
juice of ½ lemon

LEMON SOUR CREAM

zest and juice of ½ lemon
¼ cup sour cream

TO SERVE

3 tablespoons chopped parsley

PREHEAT oven to 220°C. Preheat two oven trays (or pizza stones).

1 Mix canned tomatoes, garlic and olive oil in a medium bowl. Season with salt and pepper.

2 Lay two sheets of baking paper on the bench and place a pizza base on top of each. Spread some tomato mixture over each base, leaving a bit of a border for the crust. Sprinkle over onion and arrange cherry tomatoes on top, cut-side-up. Sprinkle over mozzarella.

3 Carefully lift up the baking paper with the pizzas on top and place on preheated trays (or stones) then carefully slide baking paper away (use a fish slice to help with this). Cook pizzas until bases are crisp and golden around the edges, 10–12 minutes. Swap position of trays halfway through cooking time so they cook evenly.

4 While pizza is cooking prepare salad. Use a vegetable peeler to peel courgettes into ribbons, stopping once you get to the core. Finely slice core. Combine courgette, parsley and cranberries in a large bowl with lemon juice and season with salt and pepper. Drizzle with extra virgin olive oil.

5 Flake salmon away from skin, discarding any remaining pin bones. Remove pizzas from oven and arrange flakes of salmon on top and sprinkle over capers (if using). Combine lemon zest and juice and sour cream together and dollop on top of pizza. Garnish with parsley.

TO SERVE slice pizzas into wedges and serve with courgette cranberry salad on the side.

ENERGY	2132kJ (508kcal)
CARBOHYDRATE	45.0g
PROTEIN	31.4g
FAT	21.3g

MED TIME

CRISPY-SKIN SALMON WITH SALSA VERDE AND PEARL COUSCOUS

SERVES 4–5
READY IN: 25 MINUTES
PREP TIME: 15 MINUTES
COOK TIME: 10 MINUTES

PEARL COUSCOUS
²/₃ cup pearl couscous
2 corncobs, husk and silk removed
1 Lebanese cucumber, diced 1cm
1 red capsicum, core and seeds
    removed, finely diced
1 small red onion, peeled and
    finely diced
2 tablespoons chopped coriander
    leaves

CRISPY-SKIN SALMON
600g salmon fillet (skin on), cut into
    4–5 fillets

TO SERVE
¼–½ cup salsa verde (see page 176)

BRING a large pot of salted water to the boil. Preheat BBQ hot plate to high (if using)

1 Start by making the salsa verde to go with the meal, then set aside.

2 Cook pearl couscous in pot of boiling water for 5–6 minutes or until al dente (just tender). Remove kernels from corncobs by standing cob on its end and slicing downwards with a sharp knife. When pearl couscous has about 1 minute cook time remaining, drop corn kernels into boiling water to cook briefly. While couscous is cooking, prepare salmon.

3 Pat salmon dry with paper towels, remove any remaining pin bones and season with salt on both sides. Heat a drizzle of oil in a large fry-pan on medium to high heat. Cook salmon, skin-side down, for about 3 minutes until skin is brown and crispy. Flip salmon over and cook for a further 1–2 minutes until just cooked through. Alternatively, cook on BBQ hot plate.

4 Drain pearl couscous and corn and toss with vegetables, coriander and about half the salsa verde. Season to taste with salt and pepper.

TO SERVE divide pearl couscous between plates and top with a piece of crispy skin salmon. Drizzle over remaining salsa verde.

ENERGY	2285kJ (615kcal)
CARBOHYDRATE	37.0g
PROTEIN	33.8g
FAT	36.8g

"
Fresh and delicious, lovely contrast of textures. Loved the corn in the couscous."

LINDA

ROAST KUMARA, ASPARAGUS, CORN AND FETA FRITTATA WITH WARM TOMATO RELISH

SERVES 4–5
READY IN: 50–60 MINUTES
PREP TIME: 15 MINUTES
COOK TIME: 40–50 MINUTES

ROAST KUMARA, ASPARAGUS, CORN AND FETA FRITTATA

500g orange kumara, peeled and diced 1–2cm
6 eggs (at room temperature)
½ cup sour cream
150g feta cheese, crumbled
1 tablespoon chopped thyme leaves
½ teaspoon salt
2 spring onions, finely sliced
2 corncobs, husk and silk removed, kernels sliced from cob
1 bunch asparagus (about 12 spears), trimmed and cut in half
1 cup grated cheese (e.g. tasty, colby, edam)

WARM TOMATO RELISH

1 red onion, peeled and finely diced
3 tomatoes, diced 1cm
2 tablespoons sugar
1½ tablespoons red wine vinegar
½ cup raisins
2 tablespoons tomato sauce

SALAD

juice of 1 lemon
1 teaspoon Dijon mustard
1 teaspoon runny honey
1 tablespoon extra virgin olive oil
2 baby cos lettuces

TO SERVE

1 spring onion, finely sliced

PREHEAT oven to 220°C. Line an oven tray with baking paper.

1 Toss kumara with a drizzle of olive oil on prepared tray and season with salt and pepper. Bake for 15–20 minutes, until tender. Turn once during cooking.

2 Combine all tomato relish ingredients (except tomato sauce) in a medium pot on medium heat and bring to the boil. Reduce heat to low to medium and simmer for about 15 minutes, stirring regularly. Add tomato sauce, season with salt and pepper and simmer for a further 5 minutes.

3 In a large bowl, whisk eggs and sour cream together until smooth. Stir in feta, thyme and salt and season with pepper.

4 Heat a drizzle of oil in a large, oven-proof, heavy-based fry-pan on medium heat. Fry spring onions for 1 minute until softened. Remove from heat, then add roasted kumara and corn kernels. Reserve about 8 pieces of asparagus to arrange on top and add remainder to pan. Pour over egg mixture. Arrange reserved asparagus spears on top. Give pan a little shake to distribute mixture evenly. Sprinkle with cheese and bake for about 20 minutes or until frittata is set. Stand frittata in pan for 5 minutes before cutting into wedges. If you don't have an oven-proof fry-pan, cook frittata in a greased, medium baking dish. In this instance it is not necessary to fry spring onions; just sprinkle them on top and bake for 25–30 minutes.

5 In a small bowl whisk together lemon juice, mustard, honey and olive oil. Chop each lettuce lengthways into wedges.

TO SERVE divide frittata between plates, dollop with warm tomato relish and garnish with spring onion. Drizzle lettuce with dressing and serve on the side.

ENERGY		2747kJ (654kcal)
CARBOHYDRATE		64.9g
PROTEIN		28.3g
FAT		30.1g

MORE TIME
GLUTEN FREE

VEG

LEMON CHILLI PAPPARDELLE WITH ROASTED BEETROOT, CHERRY TOMATOES AND COURGETTES

SERVES 4–5
READY IN: 30 MINUTES
PREP TIME: 15 MINUTES
COOK TIME: 15 MINUTES

GARLIC CHILLI OIL
¼ cup extra virgin olive oil
1 red chilli, finely chopped
6 cloves garlic, finely sliced

PAPPARDELLE
2 bunches (8–10) baby beetroot,
  scrubbed and quartered (or use
  2 normal-sized beetroot, peeled
  and diced 3cm)
4 courgettes
1 red onion, thinly sliced
2 punnets cherry tomatoes
400g fresh or dried pappardelle
  (or tagliatelle or fettucine)
zest and juice of 3 lemons
1 cup chopped basil leaves

TO SERVE
100g shaved or finely grated
  parmesan cheese
½ cup toasted pine nuts*
handful basil leaves

PREHEAT oven to 200°C. Line an oven tray with baking paper. Bring a large pot of salted water to the boil.

1 Combine all garlic chilli oil ingredients in a small pot on low heat. Allow oil to gently warm and infuse for 10 minutes (it will simmer lightly). Do not let oil get too hot otherwise garlic and chilli will burn.

2 Toss beetroot with a drizzle of olive oil on prepared tray. Season with salt and pepper and roast for 15 minutes until tender.

3 Use a vegetable peeler to peel ribbons from courgettes, stopping when you get to the core, then thinly slice the core into rounds.

4 Heat a drizzle of olive oil in a large fry-pan on medium heat. Cook onion and sliced courgette rounds (but not ribbons) for 2–3 minutes until onion is starting to caramelise and courgette is lightly browned. Add cherry tomatoes and cook for a further 2–3 minutes until tomatoes are soft. Prick them with a fork to help them release their juices. Add courgette ribbons and cook for a further minute, then turn off heat.

5 Shake pasta to separate strands (if using fresh pasta) and add to pot of boiling water, stir and cook for 2–3 minutes (or according to packet instructions) until al dente (just tender). Scoop out about ¼ cup pasta cooking water and reserve, then drain pasta. Tip drained pasta and roasted beetroot back into pan with vegetables, along with chilli garlic oil, lemon zest and juice and basil. Toss together. If pasta is looking a little dry, add 2–3 tablespoons reserved pasta cooking water. Season to taste with salt and pepper.

TO SERVE divide lemon chilli pappardelle between bowls. Scatter over parmesan, pine nuts and basil leaves.

*TIP
Toast pine nuts in a small, dry fry-pan on medium heat for 1-2 minutes until light golden, moving pan frequently to avoid burning.

ENERGY	2722kJ (648kcal)
CARBOHYDRATE	65.2g
PROTEIN	26.4g
FAT	30.5g

> Lovely light seasonal meal. Yum."
>
> **TRACEY**

MY RUSTIC
AUTUMN
RECIPES

COUSCOUS-CRUSTED FISH WITH ROAST VEGETABLE SALAD AND HONEY MUSTARD MAYO

SERVES 4–5
READY IN: 50 MINUTES
PREP TIME: 25 MINUTES
COOK TIME: 25 MINUTES

COUSCOUS-CRUSTED FISH

1 ½ cups boiling water
1 ½ cups couscous
600g boneless, skinless white
   fish fillets
¼ teaspoon salt
zest of 1 lemon
½ cup flour seasoned with
   ½ teaspoon salt
1 egg
½ cup milk
1–2 tablespoons olive oil

ROAST VEGETABLE SALAD

800g butternut, peeled and
   diced 1–2cm
1 tablespoon olive oil
1 punnet cherry tomatoes
2–3 handfuls baby spinach leaves,
   roughly chopped
½ red onion, finely diced

HONEY MUSTARD MAYO

¼ cup mayonnaise
juice of 1 lemon
2 teaspoons Dijon mustard
2 teaspoons runny honey

TO SERVE

1 lemon, cut into wedges
½ cup chopped parsley

PREHEAT oven to 220°C. Line an oven tray with baking paper. Bring a full kettle to the boil.

1 In a large, heat-proof bowl, combine boiling water and couscous. Stir, cover and leave to swell for 5 minutes, then fluff up grains with a fork. Spread out on a large tray to cool in the fridge for 5 minutes.

2 Toss butternut with oil on prepared tray and season with salt and pepper. Roast for about 15 minutes then add cherry tomatoes and cook for a further 5–8 minutes until tomatoes blister and butternut is tender. Toss through spinach and red onion.

3 Pat fish dry with paper towels and remove any remaining scales or bones. Cut any larger fillets in half and sprinkle with salt and lemon zest. Place seasoned flour in a shallow dish, and whisk egg and milk in a second dish. Coat each piece of fish first in flour, then egg mixture, then with cooled couscous. Press down on couscous to coat well. Set aside on a plate and place in the fridge to set for a few minutes.

4 In a small bowl combine all honey mustard mayo ingredients and whisk well with a fork.

5 Heat oil in a large fry-pan (preferably non-stick) on medium heat and cook fish, in batches, for about 3 minutes each side, or until golden, crispy and cooked through. Take care not to burn the couscous, reducing heat if needed.

TO SERVE place roast vegetable salad onto plates, top with fish and drizzle with honey mustard mayo. Squeeze over lemon juice and sprinkle over parsley.

ENERGY	2544kJ (606kcal)
CARBOHYDRATE	58.7g
PROTEIN	38.4g
FAT	23.4g

 use egg instead of milk

"Absolutely delicious —
have never used couscous
to crumb fish before, but
it was really easy and
made the dish!"

HELEN

"Delicious soup.
Loved the croutons —
something different
that I wouldn't have
thought to add."

BECKS

MINESTRONE SOUP WITH PARMESAN SOURDOUGH CROUTONS

SERVES 4–5
READY IN: 50 MINUTES
PREP TIME: 15 MINUTES
COOK TIME: 35 MINUTES

MINESTRONE SOUP

2 tablespoons olive oil
1 onion, finely diced
2 cloves garlic, minced
1 carrot, peeled and diced
2 stalks celery, diced
250g streaky bacon, diced
½ cup red wine
2 x 400g cans crushed tomatoes
2 tablespoons chopped oregano
   leaves
1 teaspoon chopped thyme leaves
3 cups chicken or vegetable stock
¾ cup orzo or risoni pasta (or use
   any small dried pasta)
3–4 handfuls chopped silverbeet
   leaves (or spinach)

PARMESAN SOURDOUGH
CROUTONS

3–4 thick slices sourdough bread,
   diced 3cm
2 tablespoons olive oil
½ cup finely grated parmesan
   cheese

TO SERVE

½ cup finely grated parmesan
   cheese
¼ cup chopped parsley

PREHEAT oven to 200°C. Line an oven tray with baking paper.

1 Heat oil in a large pot on medium heat. Cook onion, garlic, carrot, celery and bacon for 3–4 minutes until vegetables have softened.

2 Add red wine, tomatoes, herbs and stock and simmer for 15–20 minutes until vegetables are cooked through. Add pasta and continue cooking for about 10 minutes, until pasta is al dente (just tender). Stir through silverbeet or spinach in the last 5 minutes of cook time. Season to taste with salt and pepper.

3 While soup is cooking, toss bread with olive oil and parmesan cheese on prepared tray. Bake for 10 minutes until golden and crispy.

TO SERVE ladle soup into bowls and top with parmesan sourdough croutons. Garnish with extra parmesan and parsley.

ENERGY	2422kJ (577kcal)
CARBOHYDRATE	39.0g
PROTEIN	23.4g
FAT	33.4g

 omit parmesan

TOFU, BLACK BEAN AND MUSHROOM SLIDERS WITH CARAMELISED ONIONS

SERVES 4–5
READY IN: 45 MINUTES
PREP TIME: 25 MINUTES
COOK TIME: 25 MINUTES

TOFU, BLACK BEAN PATTIES

1 x 400g can black beans, drained
 and rinsed
200g firm tofu
1 carrot, peeled and grated
¼ onion, very finely diced or grated
125g portobello mushrooms,
 very finely chopped
1 teaspoon lemon pepper
1 teaspoon paprika
1 clove garlic, minced
¼ cup chopped mint leaves
2 tablespoons soy sauce
½ cup quick cook oats
¼ cup fine breadcrumbs
1 egg

CARROT AND PARSNIP CHIPS

2–3 parsnips, cut into 2cm thick chips
2 carrots, cut into 2cm thick chips

MUSHROOMS

knob of butter
125g portobello mushrooms,
 thinly sliced

TO SERVE

8–10 slider buns, cut in half
 horizontally (or 4–5 large
 burger buns)
¼ cup mayonnaise
2 tomatoes, thinly sliced
½ cup caramelised onions
 (store-bought or see page 180)
lettuce leaves

PREHEAT oven to 200°C. Line two oven trays with baking paper.

1 Place beans in a large bowl and roughly mash until most have been crushed. Using your hands and a paper towel, squeeze moisture out of tofu, breaking it up slightly as you squeeze it. Crumble tofu into bean mixture. Add all remaining tofu black bean patty ingredients, season with pepper and mix well using clean hands. If the mixture is too moist, add more oats and breadcrumbs (up to ¼ cup more of each) until the consistency is firm enough to shape – how wet the mixture will be depends on the tofu. Set aside for 5 minutes to allow mixture to firm up slightly.

2 Toss parsnips and carrots with a drizzle of oil on first prepared tray. Bake for 20–25 minutes until golden and cooked through. Turn once during cooking.

3 Use a quarter cup measure to scoop out patty mixture and roll into large balls. Shape into patties, about the size to fit slider buns. If using large buns, use a half cup measure per patty.

4 Heat a drizzle of oil in a large, non-stick fry-pan on medium heat. Cook patties, in batches, for 2–3 minutes each side until golden brown. Use a fish slice to push down on patties to ensure a crust is formed. Transfer to second prepared tray. Place burger buns, cut-side-up, on tray next to patties and place in oven for 5 minutes until buns are lightly golden and patties are warmed through.

5 In same pan patties were cooked in, heat butter on medium heat and cook mushrooms for 1–2 minutes each side until softened.

TO SERVE spread top half of each bun with mayonnaise. Place tofu black bean patty on bottom half with sliced tomato, caramelised onions, mushrooms and lettuce. Serve with carrot and parsnip chips.

ENERGY	2313kJ (551kcal)
CARBOHYDRATE	63.5g
PROTEIN	22.7g
FAT	19.7g

   use oil instead of butter

"Really fantastic vege burgers. The patties were tasty and looked like 'normal' burgers."

KAY

This was delicious,
all went together well.
Really enjoyed the
mango in the salad!"

BRONWEN

STICKY PORK RIBS, SWEET CHILLI WEDGES AND MANGO SPINACH SALAD

SERVES 5
READY IN: 2 HOURS
PREP TIME: 20 MINUTES
COOK TIME: 1 HOUR 35 MINUTES

STICKY PORK RIBS

1.5kg pork spare ribs
½ cup hoisin sauce
½ cup water or apple juice
¼ cup soy sauce
¾ teaspoon Chinese five-spice
¾ teaspoon smoked paprika
¼ cup tomato sauce
3cm piece ginger, sliced

SWEET CHILLI WEDGES

600g mixed kumara (red, orange
   and golden), scrubbed (leave
   skin on) and cut into 2cm thick
   wedges
2–3 teaspoons olive oil
2 tablespoons sweet chilli sauce

MANGO SPINACH SALAD

3 large handfuls baby spinach
   leaves
1 mango, peeled and thinly sliced
3 cups finely shredded cabbage
¼ cup chopped coriander leaves
1–2 tablespoons toasted black
   and white sesame seeds*
juice of 1 lemon or lime

TO SERVE

1 lemon or lime, cut into wedges
a few coriander leaves

PREHEAT oven to 180°C. Line an oven tray with baking paper.

1 Cut pork ribs up by slicing through every second rib. In a deep oven tray or casserole dish, combine all remaining sticky pork ribs ingredients. Mix well to coat the ribs. Cover with baking paper, then wrap tightly with foil or cover with a lid and bake for 1 hour 15 minutes.

2 Remove foil or lid and baking paper, and increase oven temperature to 200°C. Cook ribs, uncovered, for a further 15–20 minutes or until tender.

3 Toss kumara wedges with a drizzle of oil and sweet chilli sauce on prepared tray and season with salt and pepper. Bake at 200°C until cooked through and caramelised, about 20 minutes.

4 Toss all salad ingredients together, with a drizzle of sesame oil.

TO SERVE pile ribs on a plate, with sweet chilli wedges and a large bowl of salad on the side, for everyone to help themselves. Drizzle braising liquid over ribs. Squeeze over lemon or lime juice just before eating, and garnish with coriander.

*TIP

Toast sesame seeds in a small, dry fry-pan on medium heat for 30–60 seconds until white seeds are light golden, moving pan frequently to avoid burning.

ENERGY	3230kJ (769kcal)
CARBOHYDRATE	53.9g
PROTEIN	58.9g
FAT	29.6g

BUTTERNUT AND LEEK RISOTTO WITH MUSHROOMS, SAGE AND CRISPY BACON

SERVES 5
READY IN: 50 MINUTES
PREP TIME: 20 MINUTES
COOK TIME: 30 MINUTES

BUTTERNUT AND LEEK RISOTTO
600g peeled butternut, peeled
    and diced 1cm
1 tablespoon butter
1 leek (white and pale green part
    only), finely diced
3–4 cloves garlic, minced
2 cups Arborio risotto rice
1 cup white wine
4 cups chicken stock
¾ cup finely grated parmesan
    cheese
½ cup sour cream
½ teaspoon salt
1 teaspoon freshly ground
    black pepper

**MUSHROOMS, SAGE
AND CRISPY BACON**
1 tablespoon butter
¼ cup sage leaves
250g streaky bacon, diced 1cm
250g portobello mushrooms, thinly
    sliced

TO SERVE
grated parmesan cheese
    (optional)
1 lemon, cut into wedges (optional)
leafy green salad

PREHEAT oven to 200°C. Line an oven tray with baking paper.

1 Toss butternut with a drizzle of olive oil on prepared tray. Season with salt and pepper and roast for 15 minutes until just cooked through.

2 Melt butter in a large pot on low to medium heat. Add leek and cook for 3–4 minutes until translucent. Add garlic and cook for a further minute. Add rice and cook, while stirring, until glistening, about 2 minutes. Add wine and stir until it is nearly all absorbed by the rice, about 2 minutes. Add stock, stir, cover with a lid and reduce to the lowest heat. Leave to cook for 15–18 minutes, stirring occasionally until rice is tender and liquid has absorbed (if risotto dries out too quickly, add ½–1 cup extra water). Add parmesan, sour cream, salt and pepper, and stir to combine.

3 While risotto is cooking, heat butter and a drizzle of olive oil in a medium fry-pan on low heat. Briefly cook sage leaves until crisp, 10–20 seconds, and set aside on a paper towel. Add extra butter to pan if required, and increase heat to medium. Add bacon and cook until beginning to caramelise, 4–5 minutes. Set aside on a paper towel. Add mushrooms and cook for 2–3 minutes, then remove from pan and set aside. Gently stir cooked butternut through risotto.

TO SERVE spoon risotto onto plates or into bowls. Top with a spoonful of mushrooms and bacon and sprinkle over some crispy sage leaves. Garnish with extra parmesan and a wedge of lemon, if desired. Serve with a leafy green salad on the side.

ENERGY	2954kJ (703kcal)
CARBOHYDRATE	70.2g
PROTEIN	25.7g
FAT	29.5g

"I wasn't sure about this at first but one bite in and I was hooked. I had to force myself to put the leftovers in the fridge before I ate the lot!"

JANINE

"
I'm going to make
these again — they
were just delish! Never
had haloumi before
and now I make sure
it's in the fridge."
NICK

CHILLI AND HERB HALOUMI ROLLS WITH BUTTERNUT TABBOULEH

SERVES 5
READY IN: 50 MINUTES
PREP TIME: 20 MINUTES
COOK TIME: 30 MINUTES

BUTTERNUT TABBOULEH

1 cup bulgur wheat
500g butternut, peeled and diced 1cm
1 punnet cherry tomatoes, cut in half
½ telegraph cucumber, diced 1cm
1 red, yellow or orange capsicum,
    core and seeds removed,
    diced 1cm
1 small red onion, finely diced
150g baby spinach leaves, roughly
    chopped
½ cup herb vinaigrette (see page 179)

CHILLI AND HERB HALOUMI ROLLS

400g haloumi cheese
1 red chilli, diced (seeds removed for
    less heat)
2 teaspoons lemon zest
2 tablespoons herb vinaigrette (see
    page 179)
10 sheets filo pastry
1–2 tablespoons melted butter, olive
    oil or olive oil spray for brushing
1 teaspoon sumac (optional)

PREHEAT oven to 200°C. Line two oven trays with baking paper. Bring a full kettle to the boil.

1 Start by making the herb vinaigrette (see page 179).

2 Place bulgur wheat in a large, heat-proof bowl and pour over boiling water to cover. Cover and leave to soak for 15–18 minutes until grains are tender.

3 Toss butternut with a drizzle of olive oil on first prepared tray and season with salt. Roast for about 15 minutes or until just cooked through.

4 Slice haloumi into fingers. To do this slice the whole piece of haloumi in half horizontally, then slice from the shorter end into ½–1cm thick fingers. You should end up with about 10 pieces. Mix chilli, lemon zest and herb vinaigrette in a bowl. Add haloumi fingers and toss to coat. Season with freshly ground black pepper.

5 Place a sheet of filo pastry on a clean bench with the short side towards you. Lightly brush or spray with butter or oil. Place 2 pieces of haloumi side by side horizontally in the middle of the bottom section of the filo. Roll up 2–3 times then fold the left and right sides inwards. Continue rolling upwards until you have a parcel. Place seam-side down on second prepared tray. Repeat with remaining filo sheets and haloumi. Brush tops of each parcel with butter or olive oil and sprinkle sumac on top, if using. Bake for 10–12 minutes or until crispy and golden. Turn tray around during cooking to ensure even browning.

6 Drain bulgur wheat and toss with remaining tabbouleh ingredients and roasted butternut.

TO SERVE divide tabbouleh between plates and top with haloumi rolls.

ENERGY	2838kJ (676kcal)
CARBOHYDRATE	54.2g
PROTEIN	26.1g
FAT	38.3g

 MORE TIME   VEG

PAPRIKA AND FENNEL PORK WITH KUMARA SALAD, YOGHURT AND MAPLE DATES

SERVES 4–5
READY IN: 30 MINUTES
PREP TIME: 15 MINUTES
COOK TIME: 15 MINUTES

KUMARA SALAD

800g red kumara, scrubbed (leave
skin on) and diced 1–2cm
2 fennel bulbs, halved lengthways
and finely sliced
3 stalks celery, finely sliced on
an angle
2 lemons, peeled, deseeded and
finely diced
¼ cup chopped coriander leaves
¼ cup chopped mint leaves
½ cup roasted, chopped
cashew nuts
½ cup natural unsweetened
yoghurt
2 teaspoons extra virgin olive oil

MAPLE DATES

80g pitted dates, halved
lengthways
¼ cup maple syrup
¼ cup red wine vinegar

PAPRIKA AND FENNEL PORK

2 teaspoons fennel seeds
2 teaspoons paprika
1 tablespoon olive oil
600g pork fillet (at room
temperature)

TO SERVE

¼ cup coriander leaves

PREHEAT oven to 200°C. Line an oven tray with baking paper. Preheat BBQ hot plate to medium (if using).

1 Toss kumara with a drizzle of olive oil on prepared tray and season with salt and pepper. Roast for about 15 minutes until golden and tender. Remove from oven and set aside to cool.

2 While kumara is cooking, prepare the rest of the meal. In a small pot on medium heat, bring all maple dates ingredients to the boil. As soon as liquid boils, remove from heat and set aside.

3 Place fennel, celery, lemon and herbs in a large bowl with cashew nuts. In a small bowl mix yoghurt with olive oil and set aside.

4 In a medium bowl mix fennel seeds and paprika with olive oil. Pat pork dry with paper towels. Slice into 3cm thick medallions, then season with salt. Coat well in spice mix. Heat a drizzle of oil in a large fry-pan on medium heat. Cook pork for about 2 minutes each side or until cooked medium. Alternatively, cook on a BBQ hot plate. Set aside to rest, covered with foil, for a few minutes.

5 Add kumara to salad and fold through yoghurt mixture to combine. Season to taste with salt and pepper.

TO SERVE spoon kumara salad onto plates. Add pork medallions, top with dates and drizzle a little date liquid over. Garnish with coriander.

ENERGY	2670kJ (636kcal)
CARBOHYDRATE	74.4g
PROTEIN	34.8g
FAT	20.2g

"Baked beans and crumble were absolutely delicious! Twelve out of ten."

LEONIE

LAMB STEAKS WITH HOMEMADE BAKED BEANS AND COURGETTE CRUMBLE

SERVES 4–5
READY IN: 45 MINUTES
PREP TIME: 15 MINUTES
COOK TIME: 30 MINUTES

BAKED BEANS

1 tablespoon olive oil
1 red onion, thinly sliced
2 cloves garlic, minced
1 carrot, peeled and grated
1 teaspoon paprika
1 teaspoon ground cumin
1 teaspoon dried oregano
1 x 400g can crushed or chopped
  tomatoes
1 x 400g can cannellini beans,
  rinsed and drained
¼ cup chicken or vegetable stock
1 tablespoon sweet chilli sauce
2 tablespoons chopped flat-leaf
  parsley leaves
2 tablespoons chopped basil
  leaves

COURGETTE CRUMBLE

2 courgettes
1 cup panko breadcrumbs
½ cup finely grated parmesan
  cheese
1 tablespoon olive oil

TO SERVE

600g lamb rump or leg steaks
  (at room temperature)
2 tablespoons chopped flat-leaf
  parsley leaves
2 tablespoons chopped
  basil leaves
leafy green salad

PREHEAT oven to 190°C. Preheat BBQ grill to high (if using).

1 Heat olive oil in a large fry-pan on medium heat. Cook onion and garlic until softened, about 3 minutes. Add carrot, spices and oregano and cook for a further 2 minutes. Add tomatoes, cannellini beans and stock, reduce heat to low and simmer until sauce has thickened, about 4 minutes. Stir through sweet chilli sauce, parsley and basil. Season to taste with salt and pepper.

2 While beans simmer, make crumble. Grate courgettes directly onto a clean tea towel, then wring to squeeze out excess moisture. Mix with breadcrumbs, parmesan and oil in a medium bowl.

3 Transfer bean mixture to a medium oven dish. Sprinkle over courgette crumble to cover and grill for 15–20 minutes until crust is golden brown.

4 Wipe out same fry-pan used for beans and return to high heat with a drizzle of oil (or use BBQ). Pat lamb dry with paper towels and season with salt and pepper. Fry for about 2 minutes each side for medium-rare (depending on thickness), or until cooked to your liking. Set aside to rest for a few minutes, covered in foil, then slice thinly against the grain.

TO SERVE spoon baked beans onto plates with sliced lamb. Garnish with parsley and basil and serve a leafy green salad on the side.

ENERGY	1890kJ (450kcal)
CARBOHYDRATE	28.1g
PROTEIN	40.2g
FAT	18.5g

 MED TIME BBQ   DAIRY FREE omit parmesan   GLUTEN FREE use GF breadcrumbs

PANEER AND MUSHROOM SAAGWALA

SERVES 4–5
READY IN: 35 MINUTES
PREP TIME: 15 MINUTES
COOK TIME: 25 MINUTES

PANEER AND MUSHROOM SAAGWALA

2 tablespoons Indian spice mix
  (see page 177)
200g paneer, diced 1cm
1 onion, sliced
300g very finely chopped baby
  spinach leaves
1 cup cream
3 cloves garlic, minced
3cm piece ginger, finely grated
200g button mushrooms, thinly
  sliced
¼ cup vegetable stock
2 tablespoons tomato paste
juice of ½ lemon

VEGETABLE RAITA

1 Lebanese cucumber
1 large carrot, peeled and grated
¾ cup natural unsweetened
  yoghurt
juice of ½ lemon
¼ cup chopped mint leaves

TO SERVE

steamed basmati rice (see page
  176)
¼ cup chopped mint and
  coriander leaves
½ cup toasted sliced almonds*

1 Start by cooking the rice to go with the meal. While rice is cooking, make curry. In a medium bowl add 1 ½ teaspoons Indian spice mix (reserve the remainder) and paneer cubes. Toss to coat in spices and season with salt. Heat a drizzle of oil in a large fry-pan on medium heat. Cook paneer for 3–4 minutes, until golden brown, shaking the pan frequently so it cooks evenly. Remove from pan and set aside.

2 Reduce heat to low to medium, add onion, a little extra oil and 2 tablespoons of water to the pan. Cook for about 8 minutes until golden brown. If onion is catching and burning on the bottom of the pan, add 1–2 tablespoons more water and stir to lift it. In a medium bowl, mix spinach and cream together. If you have a stick blender, purée spinach and cream until smooth.

3 Add another drizzle of oil to pan, along with garlic, ginger and remaining spice mix. Cook for 1–2 minutes until fragrant.

4 Add mushrooms and stock, cook for a further 2 minutes or until soft. Stir in tomato paste and spinach mixture and simmer for 5 minutes until sauce has thickened slightly. Return paneer to pan and squeeze in lemon juice. Stir to combine and season to taste with salt and pepper.

5 While curry is cooking, grate cucumber into a clean tea towel and squeeze out excess moisture. Mix with carrot, yoghurt, lemon juice and mint in a medium bowl. Season to taste with salt and pepper.

TO SERVE divide rice, curry and raita between plates. Garnish with mint, coriander and almonds.

*TIP
Toast sliced almonds in a small, dry fry-pan on medium heat for 1–2 minutes until golden, moving pan frequently to avoid burning.

ENERGY	2912kJ (693kcal)
CARBOHYDRATE	46.3g
PROTEIN	23.1g
FAT	47.4g

 MED TIME GLUTEN FREE VEG

This was absolutely delicious — the flavours were spot on. I loved the edamame beans and pickled courgette."

YOLANDA

TERIYAKI CHICKEN WITH SESAME GREENS, PICKLED COURGETTE AND RICE

SERVES 4—5
READY IN: 35 MINUTES
PREP TIME: 15 MINUTES
COOK TIME: 20 MINUTES

PICKLED COURGETTE
⅔ cup rice wine vinegar
2 tablespoons sugar
1 teaspoon salt
2 courgettes, peeled into ribbons

TERIYAKI CHICKEN
¼ cup soy sauce
2 tablespoons white wine
3 tablespoons brown sugar
¼ cup water
1 teaspoon finely grated ginger
2 cloves garlic, sliced
600g boneless chicken thighs
  (skin on)

SESAME GREENS
1 teaspoon oil
2 teaspoons sesame oil
300g green beans, trimmed and
  sliced 1cm
150g frozen podded edamame
  beans, defrosted
2 spring onions, thinly sliced
zest of 1 lemon
2 tablespoons toasted sesame
  seeds*

TO SERVE
steamed jasmine rice
1 spring onion, green part only,
  thinly sliced
1 lemon, cut into wedges

1 Start by cooking the rice to go with the meal. While rice is cooking, prepare rest of meal. In a small pot, bring vinegar, sugar and salt to the boil. Remove vinegar mixture from heat and pour over courgette ribbons, cover and leave to cool in the fridge.

2 Mix soy sauce, wine, sugar, water, ginger and garlic together and set aside.

3 Heat a drizzle of oil in a large fry-pan (preferably non-stick) on medium heat. Pat chicken dry with paper towels and cook, skin-side down, for 6 minutes until skin is golden. Drain excess fat from pan, turn chicken over and add teriyaki sauce. Reduce heat to low and simmer chicken in sauce for 4—5 minutes, while spooning sauce over chicken. Add 1—2 tablespoons water if sauce is reducing too quickly.

4 Heat oil and sesame oil in a large fry-pan on medium heat. Add green beans and stir-fry for 2 minutes. Add edamame beans and spring onions and cook for a further 1—2 minutes. Season with salt and add lemon zest and sesame seeds. Drain courgettes.

TO SERVE place rice, chicken and sesame greens onto plates. Drizzle with sauce from the pan and serve with pickled courgette. Garnish with green part of spring onion and squeeze over lemon juice just before eating.

*TIP
Toast sesame seeds in a small, dry fry-pan on medium heat for 30–60 seconds until light golden, moving pan frequently to avoid burning.

ENERGY	2209kJ (526kcal)
CARBOHYDRATE	61.6g
PROTEIN	36.3g
FAT	13.7g

   use GF soy sauce

BEEF STEAKS WITH SPICED ROAST VEGETABLE SALAD AND LEMON CURRY DRESSING

SERVES 4–5
READY IN: 45 MINUTES
PREP TIME: 15 MINUTES
COOK TIME: 35 MINUTES

ROAST VEGETABLE SALAD AND BEEF

600g mixed kumara, scrubbed (leave skin on) and diced 3cm

2 carrots, peeled and diced 3cm

300g yams, halved lengthways

1 red capsicum, core and seeds removed, roughly chopped

1½ red onions, peeled and cut into 2cm thick wedges

2 tablespoons olive oil

2 teaspoons cumin seeds

2 teaspoons yellow or brown mustard seeds

1 teaspoon fennel seeds

1 teaspoon coriander seeds

½ teaspoon salt

150g baby spinach leaves

600g beef sirloin, scotch fillet or rump steaks (at room temperature)

LEMON CURRY DRESSING

1 lemon, peeled, deseeded and finely diced

¼ red onion, finely diced

2 tablespoons mayonnaise

2 tablespoons natural unsweetened yoghurt

½ teaspoon mild curry powder

¼ teaspoon ground turmeric

1 teaspoon wholegrain mustard

1 teaspoon runny honey

PREHEAT oven to 210°C. Line two oven trays with baking paper. Preheat BBQ grill to high (if using).

1 Toss kumara, carrots, yams, capsicum and onions with oil, spices and salt on prepared trays in a single layer. Roast for about 30 minutes until golden and tender. Turn once and swap trays over halfway through to ensure even cooking. Remove from oven, toss with spinach leaves and return to oven for about 1 minute, to wilt spinach.

2 While vegetables cook prepare rest of meal. Place all lemon curry dressing ingredients in a small bowl and mix well. Season to taste with salt and pepper.

3 Pat beef dry with paper towels and season with salt and pepper. When vegetables have about 8 minutes of cook time remaining, heat a drizzle of oil in a large fry-pan on high heat (or use BBQ) and cook steaks for 2–3 minutes each side for medium-rare (depending on thickness) or until cooked to your liking. Set aside to rest for a few minutes, covered with foil.

TO SERVE place roast vegetable salad and beef steaks on plates. Drizzle over dressing.

ENERGY	2456kJ (585kcal)
CARBOHYDRATE	59.0g
PROTEIN	35.5g
FAT	21.5g

    omit yoghurt

Delish — loved the
dressing. This is what
I love about your meals:
a simple dressing
transforms a meal."
DONNA

"Quick and easy to make and so very yummy. That sauce was tasty and everything just went so well together. Delicious."

SEARED VENISON WITH ROASTED KUMARA, FENNEL, APPLE AND CREAM PEPPER SAUCE

SERVES 5
READY IN: 30 MINUTES
PREP TIME: 15 MINUTES
COOK TIME: 15 MINUTES

ROASTED KUMARA, FENNEL AND APPLE

800g red kumara, scrubbed (leave skin on) and diced 1.5cm
4 red apples, core removed, cut into thick wedges
1 fennel bulb, cut into 1cm thick wedges

VENISON AND PEPPER SAUCE

600g venison medallions (at room temperature)
2 teaspoons freshly ground mixed peppercorns (e.g. red, green and black)
1–2 tablespoons butter
2 shallots, finely diced
2 cloves garlic, finely diced
½ cup white wine
1 cup cream
½ cup chopped parsley

TO SERVE

2 tablespoons flat-leaf parsley leaves
2 bunches broccolini, steamed (or any steamed greens)

PREHEAT oven to 200°C. Line two oven trays with baking paper.

1 Toss kumara, apples and fennel with a drizzle of olive oil on prepared trays and season with salt and pepper. Roast for about 15 minutes until tender. Turn once during cooking.

2 Heat a drizzle of oil in a large fry-pan on high heat. Pat venison dry with paper towels, season with salt, sprinkle with 1 teaspoon ground mixed pepper and fry for about 2 minutes each side for medium-rare (depending on thickness) or until cooked to your liking. Set aside to rest, covered with foil, for a few minutes.

3 While venison is resting make the sauce. Reduce heat to low and add butter, shallots and garlic to same pan venison was cooked in. Fry for about 3 minutes until soft then add remaining ground pepper and wine and cook for a further 2–3 minutes until wine has evaporated. Add cream and simmer for 2 minutes until slightly thickened. Remove from heat, stir in parsley and season to taste with salt and more freshly ground mixed peppercorns.

4 Slice venison thinly against the grain.

TO SERVE divide kumara, apple and fennel between plates, top with slices of venison and spoon over pepper sauce. Scatter over parsley. Serve broccolini on the side.

ENERGY	2843kJ (677kcal)
CARBOHYDRATE	61.2g
PROTEIN	37.0g
FAT	27.2g

HERB AND CITRUS PORK WITH ROAST BUTTERNUT, PEAR AND KALE SALAD

SERVES 4–5
READY IN: 35 MINUTES
PREP TIME: 15 MINUTES
COOK TIME: 25 MINUTES

ROAST BUTTERNUT, PEAR AND KALE SALAD

800g butternut (leave skin on), diced 2cm
2 red onions, cut into 2cm thick wedges
2 tablespoons olive oil
2 teaspoons runny honey
150g curly kale, tough stems removed, leaves very finely sliced
2 tablespoons extra virgin olive oil
juice of 1 lemon
2 ripe pears, cored and thinly sliced

HERB AND CITRUS PORK

600g pork fillet (at room temperature)
1 tablespoon finely chopped rosemary leaves
1 tablespoon finely chopped thyme leaves
zest of 2 lemons

DRESSING

juice of 2 mandarins
1 teaspoon wholegrain mustard
1 teaspoon runny honey

TO SERVE

2–3 tablespoons chopped roasted hazelnuts, cashew nuts or almonds

PREHEAT oven to 200°C. Line an oven tray with baking paper.

1 Toss butternut, red onions, olive oil and honey on prepared tray. Season with salt and pepper, and roast for about 25 minutes or until tender and golden. Turn once during cooking.

2 Pat pork dry with paper towels. Combine with rosemary, thyme, lemon zest and a drizzle of olive oil. Leave to marinate at room temperature while you prepare the rest of the meal.

3 Place kale in a large bowl with oil, lemon juice and a good pinch of salt. Use your fingertips to gently 'massage' the kale and set aside to marinate – this helps to soften the kale.

4 Heat a drizzle of olive oil in a large fry-pan on high heat. Season pork with salt and fry until browned, about 1 minute on all four sides. Place pork on top of vegetables to finish cooking for 6–8 minutes or until cooked medium. Set aside to rest, covered with foil, for 5–10 minutes before slicing.

5 Mix all dressing ingredients together with a pinch of salt.

TO SERVE toss roast vegetables with marinated kale and pear. Divide salad between plates, top with slices of pork, pour dressing over the pork and salad, and scatter over nuts.

ENERGY	1997kJ (475kcal)
CARBOHYDRATE	36.6g
PROTEIN	32.8g
FAT	22.9g

I absolutely loved the
textures of this salad.
Big thumbs up from us."
GABBY

"
Those balsamic tomatoes
are a revelation! And that
creamy mash was divine."

STEAK WITH BALSAMIC TOMATOES, PARMESAN OREGANO MASH AND ROCKET AND PEAR SALAD

SERVES 4–5
READY IN: 30 MINUTES
PREP TIME: 15 MINUTES
COOK TIME: 15 MINUTES

PARMESAN OREGANO MASH
800g agria potatoes, peeled and diced 2cm
2 tablespoons butter
⅓ cup milk
½ cup finely grated parmesan cheese
1 tablespoon chopped oregano or marjoram leaves

BALSAMIC TOMATOES
2 cloves garlic, finely chopped
2 tablespoons olive oil
2 tablespoons balsamic vinegar
2 teaspoons brown sugar
2 teaspoons chopped oregano leaves
2 punnets cherry tomatoes

BEEF
600g beef sirloin or scotch fillet steaks (at room temperature)
2 tablespoons olive oil

ROCKET AND PEAR SALAD
120–150g rocket leaves
2 pears, cored and thinly sliced
¼ cup shaved parmesan cheese
2 tablespoons toasted pine nuts*
balsamic vinegar and extra virgin olive oil, to dress

BRING a large pot of salted water to the boil. Preheat BBQ grill to high (if using).

1 Cook potatoes in pot of boiling water until very soft, 12–15 minutes. Drain and return to pot with butter, milk, parmesan and oregano or marjoram. Mash until smooth and season to taste with salt and pepper. Keep warm.

2 Place all balsamic tomatoes ingredients in a medium bowl and toss to combine. Season with salt and pepper and set aside.

3 Pat beef dry with paper towels, rub with olive oil and season with salt and pepper. When potatoes are almost cooked, heat a large fry-pan on high heat and fry beef for about 2 minutes each side for medium-rare (depending on thickness) or until cooked to your liking. Alternatively, cook on BBQ grill. Set aside to rest, covered with foil, for 5–10 minutes, then slice thickly against the grain.

4 Reduce pan temperature to medium. Once pan has cooled slightly, add balsamic tomatoes and stir regularly for 3–4 minutes until tomatoes have started to blister and marinade has reduced and become sticky. If marinade reduces too quickly and tomatoes start to stick, add 2–3 tablespoons water and toss to evaporate.

5 Toss rocket, pear and parmesan salad ingredients together.

TO SERVE spoon parmesan oregano mash onto plates and top with beef and balsamic tomatoes. Serve with rocket, pear and parmesan salad on the side, dressed with a drizzle of extra virgin olive oil and balsamic vinegar.

*TIP
Toast pine nuts in a small, dry fry-pan on medium heat for 1-2 minutes until golden, moving pan frequently to avoid burning.

ENERGY	2733kJ (651kcal)
CARBOHYDRATE	38.9g
PROTEIN	45.1g
FAT	34.4g

 MED TIME · GLUTEN FREE · BBQ

THAI BEEF, CARAMELISED PUMPKIN, KAFFIR LIME AND SPINACH SALAD

SERVES 4–5
READY IN: 40 MINUTES
PREP TIME: 15 MINUTES
COOK TIME: 30 MINUTES

CARAMELISED PUMPKIN

800g pumpkin, peeled and diced
   2–3cm
1 teaspoon ground cumin
1 teaspoon ground turmeric
2 tablespoons sweet chilli sauce
4 cloves garlic, finely chopped
1 tablespoon olive oil

DRESSING

2 kaffir lime leaves, central stem
   removed, very finely chopped
1 red chilli, seeds removed and
   finely chopped (optional)
1 tablespoon finely grated ginger
2 cloves garlic, minced
juice of 1 ½ lemons or 2 limes
4 teaspoons fish sauce
3 tablespoons sweet chilli sauce
2 tablespoons extra virgin olive oil

BEEF AND SALAD

600g beef sirloin or scotch fillet
   steaks (at room temperature)
½ teaspoon ground coriander
½ teaspoon ground turmeric
150g baby spinach leaves
½ cup chopped roasted peanuts
½ –1 cup chopped Thai herbs
   (e.g. coriander, mint, Vietnamese
   mint and Thai basil)

PREHEAT oven to 200°C. Preheat BBQ grill (if using). Line an oven tray with baking paper.

1 Toss pumpkin with spices, sweet chilli sauce, garlic and olive oil on prepared tray. Season with salt and roast for 25–30 minutes until caramelised. The pumpkin should be brown and a bit sticky around the edges.

2 In a small bowl, mix all dressing ingredients together and set aside.

3 Pat beef dry with paper towels. Rub all over with ground coriander and tumeric and season well with salt. Heat a drizzle of oil in a large fry-pan on high heat. Cook for about 2 minutes each side for medium-rare (depending on thickness) or until cooked to your liking. Alternatively, cook on BBQ grill. Set aside to rest for 5–10 minutes, covered with foil, before slicing thinly against the grain.

4 Toss pumpkin with spinach, peanuts, half the Thai herbs and dressing.

TO SERVE divide salad between plates and top with slices of beef. Garnish with remaining Thai herbs.

ENERGY	1958kJ (466kcal)
CARBOHYDRATE	20.9g
PROTEIN	37.3g
FAT	25.7g

MED TIME · DAIRY FREE · GLUTEN FREE · BBQ

> "Easy to prepare and great flavours. First time there has been 'negotiation' over who got to take the leftovers for lunch!"
>
> CHARLOTTE

This was a great hearty meal. So easy to prepare and I loved the overall taste."

CARMEN

LAMB TAGINE WITH DATES, PEAR AND COUSCOUS

SERVES 5
READY IN: 2 HOURS 15 MINUTES
PREP TIME: 20 MINUTES
COOK TIME: 1 HOUR 40 MINUTES

LAMB TAGINE

600g lamb leg or shoulder (or a
   mix), diced 3cm
2½ tablespoons tagine spice mix
   (see page 177)
2 tablespoons olive oil
2 tablespoons butter
2 onions, sliced 0.5cm
2 cloves garlic, minced
1 cup red wine
2 cups chicken stock
1 tablespoon runny honey
2 x 400g cans chopped tomatoes
2 pears, cored and cut into eighths
4 carrots, peeled, quartered
   lengthways, then cut in half
½ cup dried apricots
½ cup dates

COUSCOUS

1½ cups couscous
½ teaspoon salt
1 tablespoon olive oil
zest of 1 lemon
1½ cups boiling water
½ cup chopped coriander
   (leaves and stalks)
½ cup chopped parsley

TO SERVE

¼ cup sliced almonds
handful coriander and parsley
   leaves

PREHEAT oven to 160°C. If you don't have a large, oven-proof fry-pan, warm a medium casserole dish in oven. Alternatively, preheat slow cooker.

1 Pat lamb dry with paper towels and toss with 1½ tablespoons of tagine spice mix. Set aside at room temperature to marinate for 5–10 minutes or overnight in fridge.

2 Heat oil in a large, heavy-based, oven-proof pot or fry-pan on high heat. Fry lamb for about 30 seconds each side until golden. Remove lamb, leaving excess oil in pan. Then add butter, reduce heat to medium and cook onion for 3–4 minutes, until soft. Add garlic and remaining tagine spice mix and cook for a further 2 minutes, adding extra oil if required.

3 Add wine, stock and honey, bring to the boil and simmer for 10 minutes until thickened slightly. Add tomatoes, season with salt and pepper, bring back to the boil then simmer for 2–3 minutes.

4 Return lamb to pan with pears, carrots, apricots and dates. Cover and cook in oven for 1½ hours until lamb is tender, or transfer to preheated casserole dish to cook. If using a slow cooker, cook for 4 hours on high or 6 hours on low. Add a little water if sauce is looking too thick.

5 When tagine is nearly ready, bring a full kettle to the boil. Place couscous, salt, oil, lemon zest and boiling water in a large, heat-proof bowl. Stir, cover with a plate and steam for 5 minutes then fluff up grains with a fork. Stir through coriander and parsley.

TO SERVE spoon couscous onto plates, spoon over lamb tagine and garnish with almonds and extra coriander and parsley.

ENERGY	3598kJ (857kcal)
CARBOHYDRATE	70.9g
PROTEIN	32.9g
FAT	43.4g

 omit butter

SUMAC AND PISTACHIO CRUMBED CHICKEN WITH GRAPE FETA SALAD

SERVES 5
READY IN: 35 MINUTES
PREP TIME: 20 MINUTES
COOK TIME: 15 MINUTES

SUMAC AND PISTACHIO CHICKEN

2 tablespoons sesame seeds
1 tablespoon sumac
½ cup pistachio nuts, finely chopped
1 teaspoon salt
600g boneless, skinless chicken breasts

GRAPE FETA SALAD

1 telegraph cucumber, diced
200g red or purple grapes
1 small red onion, thinly sliced
100g baby spinach leaves
½ cup sliced mint leaves
100g feta cheese, crumbled
juice of 1 lemon

TO SERVE

1 small loaf ciabatta (optional)
¾ cup hummus (store-bought or see page 178)
handful mint leaves

PREHEAT oven to 200°C. Line an oven tray with baking paper.

1 Mix sesame seeds, sumac, pistachios and salt together. Pat chicken dry with paper towels and cut into steaks. To do this, place your hand flat on top of each chicken breast and use a knife to slice through horizontally to make 2 thin steaks, trying to keep equal thickness on both sides. Coat chicken well in pistachio mix.

2 Heat a drizzle of olive oil in a large fry-pan (preferably non-stick) on medium heat. Cook chicken, in batches, for 2–3 minutes each side until golden brown but not cooked through, being careful not to burn nuts. Transfer to prepared tray to finish cooking in oven for 3 minutes, or until just cooked through.

3 In a large bowl, combine all salad ingredients with a drizzle of extra virgin olive oil and season to taste with salt and pepper.

4 Warm ciabatta in oven, if using, for 3–4 minutes. Slice thickly.

TO SERVE place chicken and salad on plates with a good dollop of hummus and ciabatta on the side. Garnish with mint leaves.

ENERGY	2341kJ (557kcal)
CARBOHYDRATE	34.8g
PROTEIN	39.2g
FAT	28.5g

  omit feta omit ciabatta

"

A really delicious
variation on a family
favourite."

ROBYN

CLASSIC BEEF LASAGNE WITH SALAD

SERVES 6
READY IN: 60 MINUTES
PREP TIME: 20 MINUTES
COOK TIME: 50 MINUTES

BEEF SAUCE
1 onion, finely diced
600g beef mince (or use 300g beef
   mince and 300g pork mince)
3 cloves garlic, minced
1 carrot, diced 1cm
2 stalks celery, diced 1cm
2 tablespoons tomato paste
1 x 700ml jar tomato passata
½ cup red wine (or beef stock)
3 tablespoon Worcestershire sauce
¼ cup chopped basil leaves
¼ cup chopped oregano leaves
1 teaspoon sugar

**BÉCHAMEL SAUCE AND
LASAGNE**
2 tablespoons butter
2 tablespoons flour
2 cups milk
pinch of ground nutmeg
1 cup grated cheese (e.g. tasty
   or mozzarella)
300g fresh lasagne sheets

TO SERVE
leafy green salad
¼ cup toasted pine nuts (optional)

PREHEAT oven to 180°C

1 Heat a drizzle of oil in a large fry-pan on medium to high heat and brown mince for about 5 minutes, breaking up with a wooden spoon as it cooks. Add a drizzle more oil to pan and cook onion, garlic, carrot and celery for 4 minutes. Return mince to pan and add tomato paste, passata, wine or stock, Worcestershire sauce, basil, oregano and sugar. Simmer for about 10 minutes until thickened. Season to taste with salt and pepper.

2 Melt butter in a medium pot on medium heat, add flour and stir continuously with a wooden spoon for about 1 minute, until frothy. Add ½ cup milk while stirring constantly. Add remaining milk, ½ cup at a time, stirring constantly to avoid lumps forming. Remove from heat and whisk until smooth. Return to heat and simmer until thick, 6–8 minutes, stirring often. Remove from heat, add nutmeg and half the cheese and stir until smooth. Season to taste with salt and pepper, and set aside.

3 In a large, rectangular oven dish (about 20cm x 30cm) spread a quarter of beef sauce over the base. Cover with pasta sheets, cutting to fit if needed. Spoon over a third of remaining beef sauce then another layer of pasta sheets. Repeat for 2 more layers, finishing with beef sauce. Pour over béchamel sauce, sprinkle with remaining cheese and bake for about 30 minutes until golden. Rest for 5–10 minutes before cutting into squares.

TO SERVE place lasagne onto plates and serve with salad on the side topped with pine nuts (if using) and a drizzle of extra virgin olive oil and balsamic vinegar.

ENERGY	2310kJ (550kcal)
CARBOHYDRATE	43.6g
PROTEIN	38.9g
FAT	22.4g

MORE TIME

BUTTER CHICKEN WITH TURMERIC SPINACH RICE AND CUCUMBER MINT SALAD

SERVES 4–5
READY IN: 30 MINUTES
PREP TIME: 15 MINUTES
COOK TIME: 20 MINUTES

BUTTER CHICKEN
600g boneless, skinless chicken
    thighs, diced 2–3cm
1 onion, thinly sliced
3 ½ tablespoons butter chicken
    spice mix (see page 177)
2 cloves garlic, minced
2 teaspoons finely grated ginger
zest of 1 lemon
1 teaspoon salt
2 tablespoons butter
1 x 400g can chopped tomatoes
1 tablespoon sweet chilli sauce
juice of ½ lemon
½ cup cream
3 tablespoons natural
    unsweetened yoghurt

CUCUMBER MINT SALAD
1 telegraph cucumber, cut in half
    lengthways, then sliced
2 tablespoons chopped
    mint leaves
2 tablespoons chopped
    coriander leaves
zest and juice of 1 lemon

TO SERVE
steamed turmeric rice (see
    page 176)
1–2 naan breads (store-bought),
    cut into quarters (optional)
100g baby spinach leaves,
    roughly chopped
½ cup natural unsweetened
    yoghurt
¼ cup chopped mint and
    coriander leaves

1 Start by cooking the tumeric rice to go with the meal (see page 176). While rice is cooking, prepare curry. Pat chicken dry with paper towels and combine with onion, butter chicken spice mix, garlic, ginger, lemon zest and salt. Heat butter in a large fry-pan on medium to high heat. Cook chicken and onion mixture for about 5 minutes or until chicken and onions are starting to brown (the chicken does not have to be cooked through yet).

2 Add tomatoes, sweet chilli sauce, lemon juice and cream, and simmer for 3 minutes or until sauce is reduced slightly and chicken is cooked through. Season to taste with salt and pepper. Remove from heat and stir through yoghurt.

3 Toss all cucumber mint salad ingredients together and season to taste with salt and pepper. Warm naan bread if using.

4 Stir spinach leaves through cooked rice.

TO SERVE spoon some turmeric spinach rice, butter chicken and salad onto each plate. Top with a dollop of yoghurt and garnish with chopped fresh herbs. Serve with naan bread, if using.

ENERGY	2672kJ (636kcal)	
CARBOHYDRATE	64.1g	Nutrition based on serving
PROTEIN	35.5g	without naan breads
FAT	26.0g	

MED TIME   GLUTEN FREE   Omit naan breads

Hard to decide what was better, the yummy tapenade or the agrodolce. But together just a brilliant meal. Such a keeper!"

PAN-FRIED FISH WITH MEDITERRANEAN POTATOES AND GRAPE AGRODOLCE

SERVES 4–5
READY IN: 35 MINUTES
PREP TIME: 15 MINUTES
COOK TIME: 30 MINUTES

MEDITERRANEAN POTATOES

700–800g agria potatoes, peeled
and diced 1.5cm
½ cup olive tapenade
(store-bought)

GRAPE AGRODOLCE

2 tomatoes
½ red onion, peeled and
finely diced
2 tablespoons brown sugar
2 tablespoons soy sauce
¼ cup red wine vinegar
2 tablespoons olive oil
200g green grapes, cut in half

PAN-FRIED FISH

600g boneless, skinless white
fish fillets
½ cup flour seasoned with
½ teaspoon salt

TO SERVE

120–150g rocket leaves
½ cup chopped parsley

PREHEAT oven to 230°C. Line an oven tray with baking paper.

1 Toss potatoes with a drizzle of olive oil on prepared tray and season with salt and pepper. Roast for 30 minutes or until golden and tender. Turn once during cooking.

2 While potatoes are cooking, prepare agrodolce. Cut tomatoes in half, scoop out seeds with a teaspoon then dice flesh 1cm. Place red onion, tomatoes, brown sugar, soy sauce, red wine vinegar and olive oil in a small pot on high heat. Boil for about 6 minutes or until sauce reduces to a syrupy glaze. Remove from heat and stir through grapes.

3 Heat a drizzle of olive oil in a large fry-pan (preferably non-stick) on high heat. Pat fish dry with paper towels and remove any remaining scales or bones. Dust with seasoned flour and fry for about 1–2 minutes each side or until just cooked through.

4 Toss olive tapenade through cooked potatoes.

TO SERVE divide rocket between plates, and top with potatoes and fish. Spoon over agrodolce and garnish with parsley.

ENERGY	1926kJ (459kcal)
CARBOHYDRATE	50.3g
PROTEIN	36.0g
FAT	11.7g

   use GF soy sauce and flour

MY HEARTY WINTER RECIPES

MOROCCAN CHICKEN WITH BABY CARROT, PARSNIP AND CHICKPEA SALAD

SERVES 4–5
READY IN: 40 MINUTES
PREP TIME: 20 MINUTES
COOK TIME: 20 MINUTES

MOROCCAN CHICKEN

600g boneless, skinless chicken
thighs, sliced 1cm
2–3 teaspoons ras el hanout (see
page 177)

BABY CARROT, PARSNIP AND CHICKPEA SALAD

2 x 400g cans chickpeas, drained
and rinsed
1 bunch baby carrots, scrubbed
and tops trimmed
3 parsnips, peeled and cut into
2 x 7cm batons
1 red onion, thinly sliced
1 red chilli, thinly sliced (optional)
2 teaspoons ground cumin
2 teaspoons ground coriander
2 teaspoons runny honey
100g baby spinach leaves

CORIANDER YOGHURT

1 cup natural yoghurt
½ cup chopped coriander leaves
1 teaspoon lemon juice

TO SERVE

½ cup roasted almonds, roughly
chopped
½ cup pitted dates, roughly
chopped
½ cup chopped coriander leaves
½ preserved lemon, flesh removed
and rind thinly sliced
pinch of sumac (optional)

PREHEAT oven to 220°C. Line an oven tray with baking paper.

1 In a medium bowl, combine chicken and ras el hanout. Set aside to marinate while you prepare the rest of the meal.

2 Pat chickpeas dry with a clean tea towel. Toss baby carrots, parsnips, onion, chilli (if using) and chickpeas with cumin, coriander, honey and a drizzle of olive oil on prepared tray. Season with salt and pepper and roast until tender and caramelised, 20–25 minutes. Toss once during cooking.

3 When vegetables have 10 minutes of cook time remaining, heat a drizzle of olive oil in a large fry-pan (preferably non-stick) on medium to high heat. Season chicken with salt and cook, in batches, until browned all over and cooked through, about 4 minutes each batch.

4 In a small bowl, mix all coriander yoghurt dressing ingredients together well.

5 Remove cooked vegetables from oven. Add baby spinach leaves and toss through until slightly wilted.

TO SERVE place some carrot, parsnip and chickpea salad onto each plate. Top with chicken, almonds, dates, coriander and preserved lemon. Dollop over coriander yoghurt and sprinkle with sumac (if using).

ENERGY		2334kJ (556kcal)
CARBOHYDRATE		51.7g
PROTEIN		44.7g
FAT		20.4g

   omit yoghurt

So full of flavour and
so simple to make!"

COQ AU VIN WITH HERB CRUSHED POTATOES, BRUSSELS SPROUTS AND BACON

SERVES 4–5
READY IN: 50 MINUTES
PREP TIME: 20 MINUTES
COOK TIME: 35 MINUTES

COQ AU VIN

600g boneless, skinless chicken
   thighs
100g middle bacon, diced 1cm
8–10 shallots, halved length ways
250g button mushrooms, halved
3 cloves garlic, finely chopped
¼ cup brandy or Cognac (optional)
2 cups red wine
1 cup chicken stock
1 tablespoon tomato paste
4 thyme sprigs, 2 rosemary sprigs
   and 2 bay leaves tied
   together with string to make
   a bouquet garni
1 tablespoon cornflour mixed with
   4 tablespoons cold water

POTATOES, BRUSSELS SPROUTS AND BACON

800g baby potatoes, larger ones
   halved
¼ cup chopped parsley
¼ cup finely chopped chives
2 tablespoons butter
600g Brussels sprouts, halved
   lengthways
50g middle bacon, diced 1cm

TO SERVE

¼ cup chopped parsley

1 Pat chicken dry with paper towels and season with salt and pepper. Heat a drizzle of oil in a medium, heavy-based fry-pan or pot (with a lid) on medium to high heat. Cook chicken for 3–4 minutes, until well browned. Remove from pot and set aside.

2 Add a drizzle of oil, bacon, shallots and mushrooms. Cook until browned, 5–6 minutes. Add garlic and cook for a further minute then pour in brandy or Cognac (if using), rubbing the bottom of the pan with a wooden spoon to release any brownings. Cook until most of the liquid has evaporated.

3 Return chicken to pan with any resting juices. Add wine, stock, tomato paste and bouquet garni, and season with salt and pepper. Cover, bring to a gentle boil, then reduce to a simmer and cook for 15–20 minutes until chicken is cooked through.

4 Bring a large pot of salted water to the boil and cook potatoes for 12–15 minutes until soft. Drain, return to pot with herbs and butter, and gently crush with a fork. Season to taste with salt and pepper.

5 Bring a second large pot of salted water to the boil and cook Brussels sprouts for 1–2 minutes, then drain. Allow to dry while you cook bacon. Heat a drizzle of oil in same pot on high heat. Cook bacon for 4–5 minutes until crispy. Add Brussels sprouts and cook for 2–3 minutes, until light golden. Season to taste with salt and pepper.

6 Remove bouquet garni from coq au vin and discard, then stir in cornflour mixture. Simmer for 1–2 minutes until sauce has thickened.

TO SERVE divide crushed potatoes between plates, top with chicken, spoon over sauce and garnish with parsley. Serve with Brussels sprouts on the side.

ENERGY	2615kJ (623kcal)
CARBOHYDRATE	45.6g
PROTEIN	46.1g
FAT	18g

   use olive oil instead of butter

DRUNKEN MUSTARD AND APPLE PORK WITH MASH AND GREENS

SERVES 4–5
READY IN: 35 MINUTES
PREP TIME: 15 MINUTES
COOK TIME: 20 MINUTES

MASH
700–800g agria potatoes, peeled
   and diced 3–4cm
2 teaspoons butter
⅓ cup milk
¼ cup finely chopped chervil
   or parsley

DRUNKEN PORK
600g pork sirloin or scotch fillet
   steaks
1 tablespoon butter
2 onions, peeled and thinly sliced
2 green apples, peeled, core
   removed and sliced 0.5cm
1½ cups apple juice or apple cider
2 tablespoons wholegrain mustard
½ cup cream

CAVOLO NERO
2 bunches cavolo nero, kale,
   spinach or silverbeet, tough stems
   removed, leaves washed and
   very finely sliced
small knob of butter

TO SERVE
2 tablespoons chopped chervil
   or parsley

BRING a large pot of salted water to the boil.

1 Cook potatoes in pot of boiling water for 12–14 minutes until soft. Drain and mash with butter, milk and chervil or parsley. Season to taste with salt and pepper. Keep warm.

2 While potatoes are cooking, heat a drizzle of olive oil in a large fry-pan on medium heat. Pat pork dry with paper towels and season with salt and pepper. Cook for 2 minutes each side (depending on thickness) until golden and cooked through medium. Set aside on a plate, covered with foil, to rest. Add half the butter to the pan and cook onion for about 4 minutes until golden. Add remaining butter and cook apples until beginning to caramelise, about 4 minutes.

3 Increase heat to high and add apple juice or cider. Bring to the boil and cook until liquid has reduced by half, about 2 minutes. Stir in mustard and cream then season to taste with salt and pepper. Return pork and any resting juices to pan and toss to coat in sauce. Heat through for about 1 minute.

4 Briefly boil or steam cavolo nero, kale, spinach or silverbeet until bright green and just cooked. Drain and toss with butter. Season to taste with salt and pepper.

TO SERVE spoon some mash, greens and pork onto plates and spoon over apples, onions and sauce. Garnish with chervil or parsley.

ENERGY	2488kJ (583kcal)
CARBOHYDRATE	46.8g
PROTEIN	35.4g
FAT	27.3g

MED TIME · GLUTEN FREE

"Loved the pork cooked in the apple and onion sauce — delicious. This will become a regular."

HELEN

The mini meatloaves are a perfect ten. Super yummy and very repeatable — I will definitely make these over and over."

MINI MEATLOAVES WITH CARROT POTATO MASH AND BROCCOLI

SERVES 6
READY IN: 35—45 MINUTES
PREP TIME: 15 MINUTES
COOK TIME: 25—35 MINUTES

MINI MEATLOAVES
1 onion, finely diced
1 carrot, peeled and grated
1 parsnip, peeled and grated
300g beef mince
300g pork mince
1 egg
¾ cup panko breadcrumbs
1 tablespoon Worcestershire sauce
1 teaspoon salt
¼ cup chopped parsley
1½ cups grated tasty cheese
½ cup tomato sauce

CARROT POTATO MASH
800g agria potatoes, peeled
   and diced 2cm
2 carrots, peeled and diced 2cm
2 tablespoons butter
¼ cup milk
1–2 tablespoons finely chopped
   chives

BROCCOLI
2 heads broccoli, cut into small
   florets

TO SERVE
2 tablespoons chopped parsley
tomato sauce or chutney (optional)

PREHEAT oven to 200°C. Grease a 12-hole muffin tin (or a loaf tin measuring about 25cm x 12cm). Bring a large pot of salted water to the boil.

1 Heat a drizzle of oil in a large fry-pan on medium heat. Cook onion, carrot and parsnip until tender, about 4 minutes.

2 In a large bowl, combine beef and pork mince, egg, breadcrumbs, Worcestershire sauce, salt, parsley, 1 cup cheese and ¼ cup tomato sauce. Add cooked vegetables, season with pepper and mix well using clean hands. Press about ¼ cup of the mixture into each greased muffin tin. Alternatively press into a loaf tin. Top with remaining tomato sauce and cheese. Bake for 20 minutes (muffin tins) or 30 minutes (loaf tin).

3 While meatloaves are cooking, prepare carrot potato mash. Cook potatoes and carrots in pot of boiling water for 15 minutes, until very soft. Drain, then mash with butter, milk and chives until smooth. Season to taste with salt and pepper. Keep warm.

4 Lightly boil or steam broccoli until bright green and just tender.

5 Remove meatloaves from oven and sit, in tin, for 5 minutes before removing.

TO SERVE place 2 mini meatloaves (or slices of meatloaf) on each plate with some mash and broccoli. Sprinkle with parsley and serve with tomato sauce or chutney on the side, if using.

ENERGY	2190kJ (521kcal)
CARBOHYDRATE	40.1g
PROTEIN	36.9g
FAT	22.8g

MED
TIME

INDIAN SPICED HALOUMI AND PUMPKIN SALAD WITH CUCUMBER YOGHURT AND GARLIC NAAN

SERVES 5
READY IN: 45 MINUTES
PREP TIME: 20 MINUTES
COOK TIME: 25 MINUTES

WARM HALOUMI AND PUMPKIN SALAD

200g yams, halved lengthways
2 tablespoons Indian spice mix
  (see page 177)
500g pumpkin, peeled and
  diced 1cm
1 x 400g can chickpeas, drained
  and rinsed
300g haloumi cheese, diced 1cm
3–4 tablespoons chopped
  coriander leaves
150g baby spinach leaves

CUCUMBER YOGHURT

1 Lebanese cucumber, finely diced
2 tablespoons mayonnaise
¾ cup natural unsweetened
  yoghurt
1 tablespoon sweet chilli sauce
¼ cup chopped coriander and
  mint leaves

GARLIC NAAN

1 clove garlic, minced
1 tablespoon melted butter or
  olive oil
2 naan breads (store-bought)

TO SERVE

¼ cup coriander leaves
½ cup sliced almonds
1 red chilli, finely sliced (optional)

PREHEAT oven to 220°C. Line two oven trays with baking paper.

1 Toss yams with a drizzle of olive oil and 1 teaspoon Indian spice mix on first prepared tray. Season with salt and pepper and bake for 6–8 minutes. Toss pumpkin, chickpeas, remaining Indian spice mix and another drizzle of olive oil on second prepared tray and season with salt and pepper. Remove yams from oven and toss through other vegetables. Divide whole mixture between the two trays. Roast for 6–8 minutes, then toss through haloumi and roast for a further 6–8 minutes until vegetables are tender and golden. Toss through coriander and spinach.

2 In a small bowl, combine all cucumber yoghurt ingredients and mix well. Season with salt and pepper.

3 In another small bowl, mix garlic and butter or olive oil together. Using a pastry brush or spoon, brush or drizzle oil mixture evenly over naan breads. Wrap in foil and bake for 3–4 minutes until warmed through, then cut into quarters or tear into pieces.

TO SERVE divide haloumi and pumpkin salad between plates with garlic naan on the side. Drizzle over cucumber yoghurt and sprinkle with coriander, almonds and chilli (if using).

ENERGY	2502kJ (596kcal)
CARBOHYDRATE	45.3g
PROTEIN	27.5g
FAT	33.4g

   omit naan

A flavour-packed
vegetarian dish.
I particularly like the
crispy chickpeas and
the dressing was
gobbled up fast."
KAREN

"
Full of flavour and loved by all. So quick and easy, and great for a cold night after sports training."

DENISE

MINCE AND CHEESE POT PIES WITH KUMARA SWEDE MASH AND LEMONY SILVERBEET

SERVES 5
READY IN: 50 MINUTES
PREP TIME: 20 MINUTES
COOK TIME: 30 MINUTES

KUMARA AND SWEDE MASH

600g orange kumara, peeled and
  diced 3cm
2 swedes, peeled and diced 3cm
2 tablespoons butter
¾ cup grated tasty cheese

PIE FILLING

1 onion, finely diced
2 cloves garlic, minced
1 carrot, peeled and grated
1 courgette, grated
600g beef mince
¼ cup tomato paste
1½ tablespoons soy sauce
1½ tablespoons Worcestershire
  sauce
1½ tablespoons mustard (e.g. Dijon
  or wholegrain)
1½ tablespoons flour
2 cups beef stock

LEMONY SILVERBEET

1kg silverbeet, tough stems
  removed and leaves thinly sliced
½ cup water
1 tablespoon butter
zest of 1 lemon
2 tablespoons lemon juice
¼ cup roughly chopped
  macadamia nuts

PREHEAT oven to 190°C. Bring a large pot of salted water to the boil.

1 Cook kumara and swedes in pot of boiling water for 12–15 minutes until soft. Drain and mash with butter until smooth. Season to taste with salt and pepper.

2 While vegetables cook, prepare pie filling. Heat a drizzle of oil in a large fry-pan on medium heat. Cook onion, garlic, carrot and courgette until soft, 3–4 minutes. Increase heat to high, add beef mince and cook for 3–4 minutes until brown, breaking up with a wooden spoon. Add tomato paste, soy sauce, Worcestershire sauce and mustard, stirring until combined. Sprinkle over flour, stir to combine and cook for 1–2 minutes. Add beef stock, stir and simmer for 5–7 minutes until thickened. Season to taste with salt and pepper.

3 Half fill 5 large ramekins (1 cup capacity) with filling or use one large pie dish. Spoon mash over to cover, rough up the surface with a fork and sprinkle over cheese. Bake for 10 minutes then change the setting to grill and cook for about 3 minutes until cheese is golden and bubbly. Remove from oven and rest for 5 minutes.

4 When pies are almost cooked, place silverbeet and water in a large fry-pan or pot on high heat and cover. Bring to the boil and cook until wilted and just tender, 2–3 minutes. Drain excess water and toss through butter, a drizzle of olive oil, lemon zest and juice, and chopped macadamia nuts. Season to taste with salt and pepper.

TO SERVE place individual ramekins (or serve spoonfuls) of mince and cheese pie onto plates. Serve lemony silverbeet on the side.

ENERGY	2581kJ (615kcal)
CARBOHYDRATE	40.0g
PROTEIN	42.3g
FAT	29.9g

MORE TIME

CREAMY CHICKEN, BACON AND LENTIL SOUP WITH CIABATTA

SERVES 4–5
READY IN: 45 MINUTES
PREP TIME: 15 MINUTES
COOK TIME: 30 MINUTES

CREAMY CHICKEN, BACON AND LENTIL SOUP

250g streaky bacon, sliced 1cm
1 onion, finely diced
2 carrots, peeled and finely diced or grated
3 stalks celery, finely diced
1 leek, white and pale green part only, thinly sliced
450g boneless, skinless chicken thighs
1–2 tablespoons chopped thyme leaves
½ cup split red lentils
2 cups chicken stock
2 cups water
¾ teaspoon salt
¼ cup sour cream

CHIPOTLE SOUR CREAM

¼ cup sour cream
1 tablespoon chipotle sauce (store-bought) or your favourite chilli sauce (optional)
1 tablespoon chopped parsley

TO SERVE

2 tablespoons chopped parsley
warmed or toasted ciabatta slices
pinch of paprika or smoked paprika (optional)

1 Heat a drizzle of oil in a large pot on medium to high heat. Add bacon and cook for about 2 minutes. Reduce heat to medium and add onion, carrots, celery and leek. Stir, cover and cook for 4–5 minutes, stirring occasionally until vegetables are just tender.

2 Pat chicken dry with paper towels and season with salt. Add to pot with thyme, lentils, stock, water and salt and bring to a simmer while stirring. Reduce heat to low, cover and simmer gently for 15–20 minutes until chicken is cooked and lentils are tender.

3 In a small bowl mix all chipotle sour cream ingredients together.

4 Using a slotted spoon, remove chicken from soup, roughly dice or shred and return to pot. Stir in sour cream and season to taste with salt and pepper.

TO SERVE ladle soup into bowls, add a dollop of chipotle sour cream and sprinkle with parsley and paprika (if using). Serve with ciabatta on the side.

ENERGY	2266kJ (540kcal)
CARBOHYDRATE	32.6g
PROTEIN	38.8g
FAT	27.6g

 omit ciabatta

"
Very filling and
flavoursome. A big
hit with the family."
TRACEY

"I have always been too scared to make fish curry but we loved this meal with its combination of colours and textures."

LYNLEY

FISH CURRY WITH COCONUT RICE AND MUNG BEAN BOK CHOY SALAD

SERVES 4–5
READY IN: 35 MINUTES
PREP TIME: 15 MINUTES
COOK TIME: 25 MINUTES

FISH CURRY

2 tablespoons oil
1 onion, finely diced
1 tablespoon black mustard seeds
2 teaspoons mild curry powder
1 teaspoon ground turmeric
1 teaspoon ground coriander
1 teaspoon ground cumin
¼ teaspoon chilli flakes or chilli
   powder
1 clove garlic, minced
1 tablespoon finely grated ginger
1 cup coconut cream
1 x 400g can chopped tomatoes
2 teaspoons brown sugar
juice of ½ a lemon
600g boneless, skinless white
   fish fillets

MUNG BEAN BOK CHOY SALAD

juice of ½ a lemon
1 teaspoon sugar
3 baby bok choy, white and green
   parts, thinly sliced
3 handfuls mung bean sprouts
½ telegraph cucumber, halved
   lengthways and thinly sliced
2 spring onions, thinly sliced

TO SERVE

steamed coconut rice (see
   page 176)
¼ cup chopped coriander leaves
¼ cup chopped roasted peanuts

1 Start by cooking the coconut rice to go with the meal. While rice is cooking, make the curry. Heat half the oil in a large fry-pan (with a lid) on medium heat. Cook onion with a pinch of salt for about 3 minutes or until starting to colour. Add remaining oil, spices, garlic and ginger, and continue to cook for a further 1–2 minutes, until fragrant.

2 Stir in coconut cream, tomatoes and brown sugar, and simmer for 4–5 minutes, uncovered, until sauce has reduced slightly. Reduce heat to low, stir in lemon juice and season to taste with salt and pepper. Pat fish dry with paper towels and remove any remaining scales or bones. Cut into 3cm pieces and place in curry sauce, cover and cook for 3–4 minutes or until fish is just cooked through.

3 To make the salad, place lemon juice, sugar and a drizzle of olive oil in a large bowl and whisk to combine. Add all remaining salad ingredients, toss to coat in dressing and season to taste with salt and pepper.

TO SERVE spoon coconut rice and curry onto plates or bowls. Garnish with coriander and peanuts and serve salad on the side.

ENERGY	2641kJ (629kcal)
CARBOHYDRATE	55.4g
PROTEIN	34.5g
FAT	30.2g

MED TIME · DAIRY FREE · GLUTEN FREE

BEEF CASSEROLE WITH HERBY VEGETABLES AND PASTRY PUFFS

SERVES 5
READY IN: 2 HOURS 20 MINUTES
PREP TIME: 20 MINUTES
COOK TIME: 2 HOURS

BEEF CASSEROLE AND PASTRY PUFFS

1 tablespoon olive oil
1 onion, finely diced
2 cloves garlic, finely diced
1 parsnip, peeled and diced 1cm
1 tablespoon chopped thyme
   leaves
600g diced stewing beef (at
   room temperature) (e.g. chuck,
   shoulder, blade, shin, gravy beef)
¼ cup tomato paste
1 tablespoon Worcestershire sauce
¼ teaspoon salt
1¼ cups beef stock
2 teaspoons cornflour mixed
   with 1 tablespoon water
300g flaky puff pastry

HERBY VEGETABLES

500g agria potatoes, peeled and
   diced 3cm
3 carrots, peeled, halved
   lengthways then sliced 2cm
   on an angle
2 tablespoons butter
¼ cup roughly chopped parsley
2 teaspoons roughly chopped
   thyme leaves

PREHEAT oven to 160°C. Preheat medium casserole dish (with a lid) in oven. Alternatively, preheat slow cooker.

1 Heat olive oil in a large fry-pan on medium heat. Cook onion, garlic, parsnip and thyme for about 4 minutes or until soft. Add beef, tomato paste, Worcestershire sauce, salt and stock, bring to a simmer then transfer to preheated casserole dish. Cover with a tight-fitting lid or foil and bake for 1 hour 45 minutes, or until beef is tender. Alternatively, transfer to slow cooker and cook for 4 hours on high or 8 hours on low.

2 While beef is cooking, prepare vegetables and herbs.

3 Once beef is cooked, stir cornflour mixture into beef casserole to thicken sauce. Season to taste with salt and pepper and set aside. Increase oven temperature to 200°C.

4 Place potatoes and carrots in a large pot of salted water and bring to the boil. Simmer for 10–12 minutes or until potatoes are just tender.

5 Lay out pastry, cut into 5 small squares or circles and place on an oven tray. Bake for about 15 minutes or until puffed and golden.

6 Drain potatoes and carrots well and toss with butter and herbs. Season to taste with salt and pepper.

TO SERVE spoon beef casserole onto plates or into bowls and top with a piece of puff pastry. Serve with herby potatoes and carrots on the side.

ENERGY	2498kJ (595kcal)
CARBOHYDRATE	47.4g
PROTEIN	36.1g
FAT	28.3g

"
Loved this. My daughter
made butterfly-shaped
pastry tops for us all —
cute and yummy."

NATALIE

SPICED LAMB FILLETS WITH CRANBERRY BROCCOLI COUSCOUS AND WARM TOMATO SALSA

SERVES 4–5
READY IN: 35 MINUTES
PREP TIME: 20 MINUTES
COOK TIME: 15 MINUTES

SPICED LAMB FILLETS

2 teaspoons mild curry powder
2 teaspoons garam masala
1 teaspoon ground fennel
½ teaspoon ground cinnamon
2 tablespoons tomato paste
2 tablespoons olive oil
1 teaspoon salt
600g lamb fillets (at room
 temperature)

CRANBERRY BROCCOLI COUSCOUS

1 cup couscous
2 tablespoons olive oil
1 head broccoli, florets very finely
 chopped
½ cup dried cranberries, roughly
 chopped
1 teaspoon salt
1½ cups boiling water
¼ cup chopped mint leaves
¼ cup chopped parsley
1 small red onion, finely diced
¼ cup sliced almonds

WARM TOMATO SALSA

1 red onion, peeled and finely
 diced
1 clove garlic, finely chopped
2 tablespoons tomato paste
1 x 400g can crushed tomatoes
1 teaspoon sugar
2 teaspoons balsamic vinegar

BRING a full kettle to the boil.

1 In a large bowl, combine spices, tomato paste, olive oil and salt. Pat lamb dry with paper towels and coat well in spice mix. Set aside.

2 In a large, heat-proof bowl combine couscous, olive oil, broccoli, cranberries and salt. Add boiling water, stir to combine then cover with a plate to steam for 10 minutes.

3 While couscous is steaming, make the tomato salsa. Heat a drizzle of oil in a medium pot or fry-pan on medium heat. Cook onion for 4–5 minutes until soft. Add garlic and cook for a further minute. Add tomato paste, tomatoes, sugar and balsamic vinegar, and simmer for about 4 minutes until thickened. Season to taste with salt and pepper.

4 While salsa is simmering, heat a drizzle of oil in a large fry-pan (preferably non-stick) on medium heat. Fry lamb for 2–3 minutes each side for medium-rare (depending on thickness). Cover in foil and leave to rest for 5 minutes before slicing.

5 Fluff up couscous with a fork then fold through herbs, onion, almonds and a drizzle of olive oil. Season to taste with salt and pepper.

TO SERVE divide couscous between plates, top with sliced lamb and spoon over warm tomato salsa.

ENERGY	2315kJ (551kcal)
CARBOHYDRATE	43.7g
PROTEIN	36.9g
FAT	24.7g

SUMAC LEMON PEPPER FISH WITH ROAST VEGETABLE AND DUKKAH COUSCOUS

SERVES 4–5
READY IN: 40 MINUTES
PREP TIME: 15 MINUTES
COOK TIME: 25 MINUTES

ROAST VEGETABLE AND DUKKAH COUSCOUS

2 bunches baby carrots, ends trimmed and halved lengthways
2 parsnips, peeled and cut into 1cm batons
2 red onions, cut into 1.5cm wedges
1 tablespoon maple syrup or runny honey
1 cup couscous
¼ cup golden sultanas or raisins
1 cup boiling water
½ teaspoon salt
1 tablespoon butter
150g baby spinach leaves, finely sliced
¼ cup dukkah (store-bought or see page 177)
¼ cup chopped parsley

DRESSING

2 tablespoons chopped parsley
2 tablespoons chopped mint leaves
juice of 1 lemon
2 tablespoons olive oil

SUMAC LEMON PEPPER FISH

600g boneless, skinless white fish fillets
1½ tablespoons sumac
1½ tablespoons lemon pepper
1 tablespoon butter
1 tablespoon olive oil

PREHEAT oven to 200°C. Line an oven tray with baking paper. Bring a full kettle to the boil.

1 Toss baby carrots, parsnips and onions with maple syrup or honey and a drizzle of olive oil on prepared tray. Season with salt and pepper and bake for 20–25 minutes until vegetables are slightly caramelised and tender. Turn once during cooking.

2 In a heat-proof bowl, combine couscous, sultanas or raisins, boiling water and salt. Stir, then cover with a plate and leave to steam for 10 minutes.

3 In a small bowl, whisk all dressing ingredients together and set aside.

4 Pat fish dry with paper towels and remove any remaining scales or bones. Coat lightly with sumac and lemon pepper, and season with salt. Heat butter and oil in a large fry-pan on medium to high heat. Fry fish, in batches, for 1–2 minutes each side, or until just cooked through.

5 Add butter to couscous and fluff up grains with a fork. Add couscous, spinach, dukkah and parsley to tray of cooked vegetables and toss to combine.

TO SERVE spoon roast vegetable and dukkah couscous onto plates, top with a piece of fish and drizzle over dressing.

ENERGY	2307kJ (549kcal)
CARBOHYDRATE	51.2g
PROTEIN	34.9g
FAT	21.2g

 MED TIME / DAIRY FREE use oil instead of butter

"The kids loved this! We cut
the silverbeet up fine so they
didn't notice, and the boys
even wanted seconds!"

DEBORAH

BAKED MEATBALLS WITH TOMATO SILVERBEET SAUCE AND SPAGHETTI

SERVES 4–5
READY IN: 45 MINUTES
PREP TIME: 20 MINUTES
COOK TIME: 25 MINUTES

BAKED MEATBALLS

600g lamb or beef mince
¾ cup fine breadcrumbs
2 carrots, peeled and grated
1 egg
1 tablespoon finely chopped
    rosemary leaves
1 tablespoon chopped oregano
1 onion, finely diced
1 teaspoon salt

TOMATO SILVERBEET SAUCE AND SPAGHETTI

1 onion, finely diced
2 cloves garlic, thinly sliced
1 x 700ml jar tomato passata, or
    2 x 400g cans crushed tomatoes
1 teaspoon sugar
4 cups chopped silverbeet or
    spinach leaves
¾ cup grated mozzarella cheese
400g dried spaghetti, fettuccine or
    linguine

TO SERVE

leafy green salad

PREHEAT oven to 230°C. Preheat a large casserole or lasagne-style dish in the oven.

1 Combine all baked meatball ingredients in a medium bowl and mix well using clean hands. Use a tablespoon to measure mixture and roll into golf-ball-sized balls. Drizzle preheated baking dish with olive oil and add meatballs. Bake for 10 minutes. Bring a large pot of salted water to the boil.

2 While meatballs bake, make the sauce. Heat a drizzle of olive oil in a large fry-pan on medium heat. Cook onion and garlic for 2–3 minutes until soft and just starting to colour. Add passata or crushed tomatoes and sugar. Bring to the boil then stir in silverbeet or spinach. Simmer for 2 minutes until wilted. Season to taste with salt and pepper.

3 Remove meatballs from oven and pour sauce over to cover. Sprinkle with mozzarella and bake for a further 10–15 minutes until cheese is melted and golden.

4 While meatballs are baking, cook spaghetti in pot of boiling water for 10–12 minutes, until al dente (just tender), or cook according to packet instructions. Drain and return to pot with a drizzle of extra virgin olive oil to prevent it sticking.

TO SERVE divide spaghetti between plates or bowls, and top with baked meatballs and sauce. Serve salad on the side drizzled with a little extra virgin olive oil and balsamic vinegar.

ENERGY	2835kJ (675kcal)
CARBOHYDRATE	84.6g
PROTEIN	46.9g
FAT	15.0g

 MED TIME DAIRY FREE omit cheese

PAN-FRIED FISH WITH CAULIFLOWER STEAKS, TAHINI FENNEL FARRO AND SALSA VERDE

SERVES 5
READY IN: 45 MINUTES
PREP TIME: 20 MINUTES
COOK TIME: 25 MINUTES

TAHINI FENNEL FARRO

1 cup farro
½ cup raisins
3–4 tablespoons tahini
¼ cup mayonnaise
1 teaspoon sugar
zest and juice of 1 lemon
1–2 tablespoons water
2 fennel bulbs (reserve fronds
　to garnish)
½ cup chopped parsley

CAULIFLOWER STEAKS

1 head cauliflower

PAN-FRIED FISH

600g boneless, skinless
　white fish fillets
2 tablespoons flour

TO SERVE

⅓ cup salsa verde (see page 176)
reserved fennel fronds
2 limes, cut in half

PREHEAT oven to 230°C. Line an oven tray with baking paper. Bring a medium pot of salted water to the boil.

1 Cook farro in pot of boiling water for 20 minutes, until al dente (just tender). When farro has 1 minute of cook time remaining, add raisins. Drain, rinse under cold water then drain again well.

2 To prepare cauliflower steaks, trim outer leaves, leaving stalk and core attached. Cut lengthways into 1.5cm thick steaks (with 4–5 florets per 'steak'). Place cauliflower on prepared tray, drizzle with olive oil and season with salt and pepper. Roast for 15 minutes then turn over and cook for a further 2–3 minutes until golden and tender.

3 Make the salsa verde (see page 176).

4 Pat fish dry with paper towels, removing any remaining scales or bones. Season with salt and pepper and lightly coat in flour. Heat a drizzle of oil in a large fry-pan on medium to high heat. Cook fish for 1–2 minutes each side until just cooked through. Set aside, covered with foil, to rest.

5 In a bowl combine tahini, mayonnaise, sugar, and lemon zest and juice. Stir in water to loosen dressing to a drizzling consistency. Trim fennel bulb, halve lengthways then finely slice. Add fennel, parsley and half the tahini mixture to farro and gently toss to combine. Season with salt and pepper.

TO SERVE place a cauliflower steak on each plate with tahini fennel farro. Top with a piece of fish, dollop over salsa verde and garnish with reserved fennel fronds. Serve extra tahini dressing on the side and squeeze over lime juice just before eating.

ENERGY	2771kJ (660kcal)
CARBOHYDRATE	45.3g
PROTEIN	35.1g
FAT	36.3g

 omit butter

"We really enjoyed the tahini and fennel combination, and liked the different way the cauliflower was cooked."

JANICE

> **"**
> My daughter asked if
> it was takeaways then
> proceeded to eat the lot,
> saying that they were
> the best noodles ever!
> Moist, delicious, better
> than a bought one."
>
> **DOROTHY**

CHICKEN AND VEGETABLE MEE GORENG

SERVES 4–5
READY IN: 30 MINUTES
PREP TIME: 15 MINUTES
COOK TIME: 15 MINUTES

CHICKEN AND VEGETABLE MEE GORENG

600g boneless, skinless chicken breasts or thighs
3 tablespoons oil
3 eggs
1 onion, thinly sliced
½ cabbage or wong bok (Chinese cabbage), finely shredded until you have 4 cups
2 carrots, peeled and cut into thin matchsticks or grated
3 spring onions, thinly sliced
400g pre-cooked egg noodles (the ones that come in a vacuum bag; alternatively you can use pre-cooked udon noodles)
1 tablespoon sambal paste
2 tablespoons oyster sauce
2 tablespoons soy sauce
2 tablespoons sweet chilli sauce

TO SERVE

1 iceberg or cos lettuce, finely shredded
¼ cup chopped coriander leaves (optional)
¼ cup chopped roasted peanuts
sweet chilli sauce, to drizzle
1 lemon, cut into wedges

BRING a full kettle to the boil.

1 Pat chicken dry with paper towels, cut into 1cm strips and season with salt. Heat 1 tablespoon of the oil in a wok or your largest fry-pan (preferably non-stick) on medium to high heat. Cook chicken for 3–4 minutes until browned all over and just cooked through. Set aside in a large bowl. Keep pan on heat.

2 Lightly whisk eggs in a small bowl and season with salt. Add to wok or pan, letting eggs cook and set as an omelette, about 1 minute. Set aside on a plate.

3 Add remaining oil to wok or pan, and add onion and cabbage. Stir-fry for about 2 minutes, or until cabbage begins to wilt. Add carrots and spring onions and stir-fry for a further 1–2 minutes. Set aside with chicken. Keep pan on heat.

4 Pour boiling water over noodles, stir briskly with a fork to separate strands, then drain well immediately. Add to pan with sambal paste, oyster sauce, soy sauce and sweet chilli sauce. Stir-fry for 1 minute to coat noodles in sauce. Return chicken and vegetables to pan and toss everything together until heated through, about 1 minute. Roughly slice omelette and scatter over.

TO SERVE place mee goreng on a large serving plate in the middle of the table with separate bowls of shredded lettuce, coriander and peanuts for everyone to help themselves. To eat, place mee goreng in a bowl, top with a handful of shredded lettuce, some coriander (if using), peanuts, a drizzle of sweet chilli sauce and squeeze over some lemon juice.

ENERGY	1979kJ (471kcal)
CARBOHYDRATE	37.6g
PROTEIN	44.3g
FAT	14.9g

RICOTTA DUMPLINGS IN TOMATO AND VEGETABLE SAUCE WITH CRUNCHY BRASSICA SLAW

SERVES 4–5
READY IN: 50 MINUTES
PREP TIME: 25 MINUTES
COOK TIME: 35 MINUTES

BRASSICA SLAW

4 pita breads, diced 2–3cm
2 tablespoons olive oil
200g Brussels sprouts
¼ purple cabbage
3 tablespoons mayonnaise
1 tablespoon lemon juice

RICOTTA CHEESE DUMPLINGS

350g ricotta cheese
¾ cup fine breadcrumbs
½ cup finely grated parmesan
   cheese
1 egg

TOMATO AND VEGETABLE SAUCE

1 onion, finely diced
1 clove garlic, minced
1 carrot, peeled and grated
2 tablespoons chopped oregano
   leaves
½ teaspoon paprika
1 x 700ml jar tomato passata, or
   2 x 400g cans crushed tomatoes
1 tablespoon sweet chilli sauce
¼ cup roughly chopped basil
   leaves
100g baby spinach leaves
¼ cup finely grated parmesan
   cheese

TO SERVE

¼ cup roughly torn basil leaves

PREHEAT oven to 180°C. Line an oven tray with baking paper. Grease a medium baking dish (measuring about 20cm x 30cm).

1 Toss pita breads with olive oil on prepared tray and season with salt and pepper. Arrange in a single layer, and bake for 15 minutes until golden brown. Remove from oven and set aside. Increase oven temperature to 220°C.

2 While pita breads bake, prepare dumplings. Place all ricotta dumpling ingredients in a medium bowl, season with salt and pepper and mix well until mixture comes together to form a dough ball. Place in fridge to firm up a little while you prepare sauce.

3 Heat a drizzle of olive oil in a medium pot on medium heat. Cook onion, garlic and carrot for 4 minutes until soft. Add oregano and paprika and cook for 1 minute. Add passata or crushed tomatoes and bring to the boil, then reduce heat to low and simmer for 6 minutes, stirring occasionally. Stir in sweet chilli sauce, basil and spinach, and season to taste with salt and pepper. Remove from heat.

4 Using damp hands, roll heaped tablespoonfuls of dumpling mixture into balls. Pour sauce into prepared baking dish, push dumplings into it, spaced evenly in rows; the tops of dumplings will be visible. Sprinkle over parmesan and bake for 15 minutes until cheese has melted and top of dumplings are golden. Leave to rest for 5 minutes before serving.

5 Trim stalks from Brussels sprouts. Cut in half lengthways, then finely slice. Add to a large bowl. Finely shred cabbage and add to bowl. Mix mayonnaise and lemon juice, add to bowl and toss together with crispy pitas.

TO SERVE divide ricotta dumplings and sauce between plates and serve salad on the side. Garnish with basil leaves.

ENERGY	2313kJ (551kcal)
CARBOHYDRATE	41.8g
PROTEIN	26.9g
FAT	29.6g

MORE TIME   VEG

This was so tasty and warming and hearty on a cold night."

EMMA

This was so full
of flavour and
everything worked
together really well."
KAREN

SALMON WITH CRANBERRY ALMOND CRUST, POTATOES, AND ORANGE AND FENNEL SALAD

SERVES 4–5
READY IN: 30–35 MINUTES
PREP TIME: 15 MINUTES
COOK TIME: 20–25 MINUTES

POTATOES

700–800g agria potatoes, scrubbed (leave skin on) and cut into 1cm rounds
4 teaspoons chopped thyme leaves

SALMON WITH CRANBERRY ALMOND CRUST

½ cup panko breadcrumbs
¼ cup chopped dried cranberries
¼ cup sliced almonds
2 tablespoons chopped parsley
4 teaspoons chopped thyme leaves
zest of 1 lemon
2 tablespoons melted butter
600g salmon (skin on), cut into 4–5 fillets

ORANGE AND FENNEL SALAD

2 fennel bulbs
2 oranges
¼ cup chopped parsley
150g baby spinach leaves
1 tablespoon lemon juice

TO SERVE

1 lemon, cut into wedges

PREHEAT oven to 200°C. Line two oven trays with baking paper.

1 Toss potatoes and thyme with a drizzle of olive oil on the first prepared tray, and season with salt and pepper. Bake for 20–25 minutes or until golden and crispy.

2 In a medium bowl, mix panko breadcrumbs, cranberries, almonds, parsley, thyme and lemon zest together. Stir in melted butter and season with a little salt and pepper.

3 Pat salmon dry with paper towels and remove any remaining pin bones. When potatoes have about 8 minutes of cook time remaining, turn over and place on lower rack in oven. Place salmon on second prepared tray, skin-side down. Season with salt and sprinkle crust mixture evenly on top, pressing down gently to adhere. Bake for about 8 minutes on rack above potatoes or until salmon is just cooked (it is best cooked medium).

4 While salmon cooks, prepare salad. Trim top and bottom and ends off fennel, slice bulb in half lengthways then very finely slice. Cut skin off oranges and slice flesh into segments or dice. Place in a medium bowl with remaining salad ingredients and a drizzle of extra virgin olive oil, and toss to combine. Season to taste with salt and pepper.

TO SERVE divide potatoes between plates, top with a piece of salmon and serve salad on the side. Squeeze over lemon juice just before serving.

ENERGY	2817kJ (671kcal)
CARBOHYDRATE	42.7g
PROTEIN	32.2g
FAT	40.2g

  use oil instead of butter   use GF breadcrumbs

BEEF FILLET WITH THYME, GARLIC AND PARMESAN ROAST POTATOES AND TARRAGON CREAMED SPINACH

SERVES 4–5
READY IN: 45 MINUTES
PREP TIME: 15 MINUTES
COOK TIME: 30 MINUTES

BEEF FILLET AND POTATOES

800g agria potatoes, peeled and diced 2cm
2 cloves garlic (skin on), halved
2 tablespoons chopped thyme leaves
¼ cup finely grated parmesan cheese
1 bunch broccolini, stalks trimmed
600g beef fillet steaks (at room temperature)

TARRAGON CREAMED SPINACH

1 tablespoon butter
2 cloves garlic, thinly sliced
300g spinach leaves, roughly chopped
2 tablespoons chopped fresh tarragon, or 1–2 teaspoons dried tarragon
½ cup cream

PREHEAT oven to 230°C. Line an oven tray with baking paper. Bring a large pot of salted water to the boil. Bring a full kettle to the boil.

1 Cook potatoes and garlic in pot of boiling water for 5 minutes then drain well. Toss with thyme, parmesan and a drizzle of olive oil on prepared tray and season with salt and pepper. Bake for 20–25 minutes until potatoes are golden and crispy. Turn once during cooking.

2 When potatoes have about 10 minutes of cook time remaining, place broccolini in a medium, heat-proof bowl. Cover with boiling water and leave for 5 minutes until bright green and just tender, then drain.

3 Heat a drizzle of olive oil in a large fry-pan on high heat. Pat beef dry with paper towels and season with salt and pepper. Cook for 2–3 minutes each side for medium-rare (depending on thickness) or until cooked to your liking. Remove from pan, cover with foil to rest for 5 minutes, then slice thickly.

4 In same pan, reduce heat to medium and add butter and garlic. Fry for 30 seconds until garlic is lightly coloured. Add spinach and tarragon and cook for 1 minute until spinach is just wilted. Add cream and simmer for 1 minute until reduced and sauce thickens slightly. Season to taste with salt and pepper.

TO SERVE divide potatoes and broccolini between plates, spoon tarragon spinach cream on plate and place beef on top.

ENERGY	2230kJ (531kcal)
CARBOHYDRATE	30.3g
PROTEIN	38.6g
FAT	27.6g

MED TIME / GLUTEN FREE

> "The roasted
> potatoes were great
> with the thyme
> and parmesan, and
> really tasty with
> the tender beef and
> spinach cream."

JON

This was literally the most
delicious fish I have ever eaten.
My husband is not big on fish
but he was blown away!"

ESTELLE

MOROCCAN COCONUT FISH WITH KUMARA MASH AND CAULIFLOWER ORANGE SALSA

SERVES 4–5
READY IN: 30 MINUTES
PREP TIME: 15 MINUTES
COOK TIME: 15 MINUTES

KUMARA MASH

700–800g orange kumara,
   peeled and diced 2cm
2 tablespoons butter
3 tablespoons milk

CAULIFLOWER ORANGE SALSA

1 head cauliflower, finely chopped
zest of 1 orange
juice of 2 oranges
4 tablespoons lemon juice
½ cup sliced almonds
1 red chilli, seeds removed and
   finely chopped
100g baby spinach leaves,
   finely sliced
½ cup chopped parsley

MOROCCAN COCONUT FISH

600g boneless, skinless white
   fish fillets
½ cup flour
2 eggs
¼ cup milk
¾ cup desiccated coconut
3 tablespoons Moroccan spice mix
   (see page 177)

TO SERVE

¼ cup coriander leaves
1 lemon, cut into wedges

BRING a large pot of salted water to the boil.

1 Cook kumara in pot of boiling water until soft, about 12 minutes. Drain, return to pot with butter and milk and mash until smooth. Season with salt and pepper and keep warm.

2 While kumara cooks, prepare salsa. Heat a drizzle of olive oil in a large fry-pan (preferably non-stick) on medium heat. Stir-fry cauliflower for about 5 minutes until lightly coloured and tender. Transfer to a large bowl to cool slightly. Add remaining salsa ingredients to bowl, toss to combine and season to taste with salt and pepper. Wipe out fry-pan with paper towels to cook the fish.

3 Pat fish dry with paper towels and remove any remaining scales or bones. Cut any larger fillets in half. Place flour in a shallow bowl, whisk eggs with milk in another bowl, and place coconut and Moroccan spice mix in a third bowl. Coat each piece of fish first in flour, then egg, then coconut spice mix. In same pan cauliflower was cooked in, heat a drizzle of olive oil on low to medium heat. Fry fish for 1–2 minutes each side or until crust is golden and fish is just cooked. Take care not to burn coconut crust.

TO SERVE divide kumara mash between plates, top with fish and spoon over cauliflower orange salsa. Garnish with coriander and lemon wedges to squeeze over just before eating.

ENERGY	2796kJ (666 kcal)
CARBOHYDRATE	57.4g
PROTEIN	39.7g
FAT	29.1g

 MED TIME · GLUTEN FREE · use GF flour

THAI RED CHICKEN AND PINEAPPLE CURRY WITH JASMINE TEA RICE

SERVES 4–5
READY IN: 30 MINUTES
PREP TIME: 15 MINUTES
COOK TIME: 20 MINUTES

THAI RED CHICKEN AND PINEAPPLE CURRY

2 onions, finely diced
2 stalks lemongrass, bottom 3cm
   and tough outer layer removed,
   finely chopped
1–2 tablespoons Thai red curry
   paste, depending on heat
   preference (store-bought or see
   page 178)
1 x 400ml can coconut milk
2 cups chicken stock
4 kaffir lime leaves, central stem
   removed, leaves finely sliced
1 x 425g can pineapple pieces in
   juice, drained
150g baby spinach leaves,
   finely sliced
600g boneless, skinless chicken
   breasts or thighs, sliced into
   1cm strips
juice of 1 lime
3–4 teaspoons fish sauce

TO SERVE

steamed jasmine tea rice (see
   page 176)
1 telegraph cucumber, peeled into
   ribbons with a vegetable peeler
¼ cup roughly chopped Thai herbs
   (e.g. mint, coriander, Thai basil,
   Vietnamese mint)
1 red chilli, finely sliced (optional)
1 lime, cut into wedges

1 Start by cooking the jasmine tea rice.

2 While rice is cooking, prepare curry. Heat a drizzle of oil in a large fry-pan or wok on medium heat. Fry onions and lemongrass for about 3 minutes, until softened. Add curry paste and ¼ cup coconut milk, and cook for about 1 minute, stirring constantly with a wooden spoon, until fragrant. Add remaining coconut milk, chicken stock, kaffir lime leaves and pineapple. Simmer, uncovered, for about 8 minutes, until sauce has thickened slightly.

3 While curry is cooking, prepare, cucumber, herbs, chilli, spinach and chicken.

4 Add spinach and chicken to curry and cook for 4–5 minutes until chicken is just cooked through. Stir through lime juice and fish sauce to taste.

TO SERVE spoon some jasmine tea rice and curry onto each plate, garnish with Thai herbs and chilli (if using). Serve cucumber ribbons on the side, and wedges of lime to squeeze over just before eating.

ENERGY	2295kJ (546kcal)
CARBOHYDRATE	55.9g
PROTEIN	37.4g
FAT	19.4g

MED TIME DAIRY FREE GLUTEN FREE

PAN-FRIED FISH WITH MASALA ROAST POTATOES, CAULIFLOWER AND CORIANDER MINT YOGHURT

SERVES 4–5
READY IN: 35 MINUTES
PREP TIME: 20 MINUTES
COOK TIME: 25 MINUTES

MASALA ROAST POTATOES AND CAULIFLOWER

600g agria potatoes, scrubbed (leave skin on) and diced 2cm
1 cauliflower, cut into small florets until you have 4 cups
300g yams, halved lengthways
3 tablespoons olive oil
4 teaspoons Indian spice mix (see page 177)
4 cloves garlic, minced
1 tablespoon finely grated ginger
1 tablespoon sweet chilli sauce
150g baby spinach leaves, sliced

CORIANDER MINT YOGHURT

¼ cup chopped coriander leaves
¼ cup chopped mint leaves
½ cup natural unsweetened yoghurt

FISH

600g boneless, skinless white fish fillets
2 tablespoons butter
juice of 1 lemon

TO SERVE

1 lemon, cut into wedges

PREHEAT oven to 220°C. Line two oven trays with baking paper.

1 Toss potatoes, cauliflower and yams with olive oil, Indian spice mix, garlic, ginger and sweet chilli sauce in prepared trays and season with salt and pepper. Roast for about 25 minutes until golden and tender. Turn once during cooking.

2 In a small bowl mix all coriander mint yoghurt ingredients together and season to taste with salt and pepper.

3 When vegetables have about 5 minutes of cook time remaining, cook fish. Pat fish dry with paper towels and remove any remaining scales or bones. Season with salt. Heat butter in a large fry-pan (preferably non-stick) on medium to high heat. Fry fish for 1–2 minutes each side or until just cooked through. In the final 30 seconds, squeeze in lemon juice and spoon over fish.

4 Toss spinach through cooked vegetables until wilted.

TO SERVE divide vegetables between plates and top with a piece of fish. Dollop over coriander mint yoghurt. Serve with a lemon wedge to squeeze over just before eating.

ENERGY	1897kJ (452kcal)
CARBOHYDRATE	38.2g
PROTEIN	32.6g
FAT	17.8g

   use oil instead of butter, omit yoghurt

LAMB RUMP STEAKS WITH BACON AND KALE COLCANNON AND BROCCOLI SALSA

SERVES 4–5
READY IN: 40 MINUTES
PREP TIME: 20 MINUTES
COOK TIME: 20 MINUTES

BACON AND KALE COLCANNON AND LAMB

800g agria potatoes, peeled and diced 3cm
1 teaspoon butter
150g streaky bacon, finely diced
½ red onion, diced
150g curly kale, leaves stripped from tough stalks, leaves finely sliced
1 tablespoon butter
¼ cup milk
600g lamb rump steaks (at room temperature)

BROCCOLI SALSA

1 head broccoli, florets and stems finely chopped
2 ½ tablespoons extra virgin olive oil
2 teaspoons runny honey
3 tablespoons mayonnaise
2 teaspoons balsamic vinegar
1 teaspoon white wine vinegar or cider vinegar
1 tomato, finely diced
½ red onion, finely diced or grated
2 tablespoons chopped basil

TO SERVE

handful basil leaves

BRING a large pot of salted water to the boil. Bring a full kettle to the boil.

1 Cook potatoes in pot of boiling water until soft, 12–15 minutes. Drain, return to pot, cover and keep warm.

2 While potatoes cook, prepare the rest of the meal. Place broccoli in a medium, heat-proof bowl with a pinch of salt and cover with boiling water. Leave for 3 minutes until just tender, then drain and set aside.

3 Heat first measure of butter and a drizzle of oil in a large fry-pan on medium heat. Cook bacon for 2–3 minutes until browned and slightly crispy. Add onion and cook for 1–2 minutes until softened. Add kale and toss for 2–3 minutes until wilted. Season to taste with salt and pepper and turn off heat. Add potatoes, second measure of butter and milk, and smash up roughly with a wooden spoon. Transfer to pot potatoes were cooked in, cover and keep warm.

4 Wipe pan clean with a paper towel and return to high heat with a drizzle of oil. Pat lamb dry with paper towels and season with salt. Cook for about 2 minutes each side for medium-rare (depending on thickness) or until cooked to your liking. Set aside on a plate, covered with foil, to rest for 5 minutes, before slicing thinly against the grain.

5 While lamb rests, prepare salsa. In a medium bowl combine all remaining salsa ingredients and stir through broccoli. Season to taste with salt and pepper.

TO SERVE place a large spoonful of colcannon on each plate, top with lamb and spoon over broccoli salsa. Scatter over basil leaves.

ENERGY	2689kJ (640kcal)
CARBOHYDRATE	37.7g
PROTEIN	40.6g
FAT	37.8g

A delicious and filling
winter meal with plenty
of flavours to boot."

ALENA

ESSENTIALS

RICE

Serve ¾ cup cooked rice per person.

Perfect Fluffy Rice

Makes enough rice for 6 servings. You can halve this recipe to make enough rice for 3 people.

Combine 2 cups rice (e.g. jasmine or basmati or brown) with 3 cups water and a good pinch of salt in a medium pot. Bring to the boil, cover with a tight-fitting lid and reduce to very low heat to cook for 15 minutes (or 20 minutes for brown rice), without lifting the lid at any time. Turn off the heat and leave to steam, still covered, for a further 8 minutes, before fluffing up with a fork.

Coconut Rice

Makes enough coconut rice for 6 servings. You can halve this recipe to make enough coconut rice for 3 people.

Combine 2 cups rice (e.g. jasmine or basmati) with 1½ cups coconut milk, 1½ cups water and a good pinch of salt in a medium pot. Bring to the boil, cover with a tight-fitting lid and reduce to very low heat to cook for 15 minutes, without lifting the lid at any time. Turn off the heat and leave to steam, still covered, for a further 8 minutes, before fluffing up with a fork.

Sesame Rice

Toast 1 tablespoon sesame seeds in a small dry fry-pan on medium heat for 30–60 seconds until light golden, moving pan frequently to avoid burning. Toss through cooked rice.

Turmeric Rice

Add ½ teaspoon turmeric and cook rice per normal instructions.

Jasmine Tea Rice

Add the contents of 4 jasmine green tea bags (rip bags open and empty contents) to pot and cook rice as per normal instructions.

WET MARINADES AND SAUCES

It's very handy having a few of these recipes up your sleeve – they can transform a meal from being mundane to anything but! These great marinades will add freshness, flavour and zing to your cooking. We've also included a couple of favourites from our last cookbook (the chermoula and Jamaican jerk marinade) which go well with any poultry or meat (the chermoula is also delicious with vegetables and seafood). If you have an abundance of herbs and make a bulk amount of any of these marinades, you can always freeze portions in small ziplock bags, ready to defrost for future use and to fast-track your meal preparation.

Harissa Marinade
Makes ½ cup

Place 3 cloves garlic, chopped, 1–2 large red chillies, chopped, 1½ tablespoons crushed cumin seeds, 1 tablespoon crushed coriander seeds, ¼ cup olive oil, 2 tablespoons tomato paste, 1 teaspoon brown sugar, juice of ½ lemon and 1 teaspoon salt in a small food processor and blitz until well combined. Alternatively bash all ingredients together in a large mortar and pestle.

Salsa Verde
Makes ½ cup

Mix together ⅔ cup very finely chopped flat-leaf parsley, 2 tablespoons very finely chopped thyme leaves, 2 tablespoons finely chopped capers, 1 small clove garlic, finely minced, 2 finely chopped anchovy fillets, juice of ½ lemon, 1 teaspoon Dijon mustard and ¼ cup extra virgin olive oil.

Chimichurri
Makes ½ cup

Place ½ cup chopped flat-leaf parsley, ½ cup chopped mint leaves, ½ cup chopped fresh oregano leaves, 5 tablespoons olive oil, 3 tablespoons red wine vinegar, 2 cloves garlic, chopped, and ½ –1 teaspoon chilli flakes in a food processor and blitz until ingredients are very finely chopped and well combined. Season to taste with salt.

Lemongrass Marinade
Makes ½ cup

Remove and discard tough outer layer from 3 stalks lemongrass and finely chop remainder. Remove and discard tough central stem from 2 kaffir lime leaves and finely chop remainder. Combine lemongrass and kaffir lime leaves with 2 tablespoons oil, 2½ tablespoons fish sauce, 2 teaspoons ground turmeric, 2 teaspoons brown sugar, 2 teaspoons minced fresh chilli or chilli paste and 2 cloves garlic, minced, in a small food processor and blitz until well combined. Alternatively bash all dry ingredients together in a large mortar and pestle then mix in wet ingredients.

Chermoula Marinade
Makes ½ cup

Place 2 cups roughly chopped coriander leaves and stalks, ½ cup roughly chopped parsley, 8 cloves garlic, zest and juice of 2 lemons, 2 tablespoons white vinegar, 2 tablespoons ground cumin, 3 teaspoons ground coriander, 4 teaspoons smoked paprika, 2 large red chillies, ½ cup olive oil and 1 teaspoon salt in a small food processor and blitz until well combined. Alternatively bash all ingredients together in a large mortar and pestle.

Jamaican Jerk Marinade
Makes 1 cup

Place 2 spring onions, chopped, 3 tablespoons chopped thyme leaves, 2.5cm piece ginger, peeled and chopped, 4 cloves garlic, 1 tablespoon ground allspice, 2 tablespoons brown sugar, juice of 2 limes, 1 tablespoon tomato paste, 1 tablespoon soy sauce, ¼ cup olive oil, 2 large red chillies and 1 teaspoon salt in a food processor and blitz until well combined. Alternatively bash all ingredients together in a large mortar and pestle.

SPICE RUBS AND SEASONINGS

Sometimes spices can make all the difference to a meal, transforming the flavours with just a teaspoon or two. Here are some of our favourite blends from Central America and the Middle East which we like to use with meat and poultry. You can always make up half cup or so of a spice mix and keep it in a jar or an airtight container to use over time.

Dukkah
Makes ½ cup

In a small dry fry-pan, on medium heat, toast 2 teaspoons each of fennel, coriander and cumin seeds until fragrant. Combine with 2 tablespoons toasted sesame seeds, ¼ cup chopped roasted almonds, ¼ cup chopped roasted pistachio nuts, 1 teaspoon sumac (optional) and ½ teaspoon chilli flakes in a large mortar and pestle and bash all ingredients together. Season to taste with salt and freshly ground black pepper.

Mexican Spice Mix

Mix together 1 teaspoon paprika, 1 teaspoon smoked paprika, 1 teaspoon ground cumin, 1 teaspoon ground coriander, 1 teaspoon dried oregano or mixed herbs, ¼ teaspoon ground chilli or cayenne pepper, and ½ teaspoon onion and garlic powder (optional).

Ras el Hanout
You can buy this popular spice blend pre-made in many supermarkets. However, if you want to make your own here is a recipe.

In a small, dry fry-pan on medium heat, toast 2 ½ tablespoons cumin seeds, 2 tablespoons coriander seeds, 1 tablespoon ground cinnamon, 1 teaspoon ground ginger, 1 teaspoon ground turmeric, and 2 teaspoons black peppercorns for around 1 minute until fragrant and darkened in colour a little. Grind toasted seeds in a mortar and pestle, or in a spice grinder.

Tagine Spice Mix

Mix together 2 teaspoons ground cumin, 2 teaspoons paprika, 2 teaspoons dried rosemary, 1 teaspoon ground turmeric, 1 teaspoon ground cinnamon, 1 teaspoon ground ginger, ½ teaspoon ground chilli or cayenne, ½ teaspoon ground black pepper and 2 teaspoons garlic powder (optional).

Butter Chicken Spice Mix

Mix together 3 teaspoons garam masala, 3 teaspoons ground cumin, 3 teaspoons smoked paprika, 1½ teaspoons ground coriander, 1½ teaspoons ground turmeric and ¼–½ teaspoon chilli powder.

Moroccan Spice Mix

Mix together 4 teaspoons paprika, 1 teaspoon ground coriander, 1 teaspoon ground cinnamon, 2 teaspoons ground cumin and 4 teaspoons sumac.

Indian Spice Mix

Mix together 2 teaspoons turmeric, 1 teaspoon garam masala, 4 teaspoons ground coriander, 2 teaspoons ground cumin, 2 teaspoons curry powder and 2 teaspoons yellow mustard seeds.

SAUCES AND PESTOS

Tartare Sauce
Makes ½ cup

Mix together 1 tablespoon chopped capers, 2½ tablespoons chopped gherkins, ¼ cup mayonnaise and zest and juice of 1 lemon.

Basil Pesto
Makes 1 cup

Place 1½ cups packed basil leaves, ½ cup packed flat-leaf parsley (leaves and stalks), ½ clove garlic, finely chopped, ¼ cup toasted pine nuts (optional), ¼ cup grated parmesan in a food processor and blitz to combine, while slowly drizzling in ⅓ cup extra virgin olive oil. Season to taste with 1–2 tablespoons lemon juice, salt and freshly ground black pepper. The pesto will keep in the fridge for a few days or can be frozen in a sealed ziplock bag for a few months

Sundried Tomato Pesto
Makes 1 cup

Place ¾ cup drained, chopped sundried tomatoes, ¼ cup, drained, pitted black kalamata olives (optional), ½ clove garlic, finely chopped, and ¼ cup toasted pine nuts (optional) in a food processor and blitz to combine, while slowly drizzling in ¼ cup extra-virgin olive oil. Season to taste with salt and freshly ground black pepper. If you don't have a food processor, very finely chop the sundried tomatoes, olives, garlic and pine nuts and mix with the olive oil. The pesto will keep in the fridge for a few days or can be frozen in a sealed ziplock bag for a few months.

Katsu Sauce
Makes ½ cup

Combine 1 tablespoon tomato sauce, 3 tablespoons Worcestershire sauce, 2 tablespoons oyster sauce and 1 tablespoon sugar until the sauce is smooth.

Hummus
Makes 1½ cups

Place 1 x 400g can chickpeas, drained and rinsed, 2 small cloves garlic, crushed, 3 tablespoons tahini (optional), and 2 tablespoons lemon juice in a food processor and blitz to combine, while drizzling in 4–5 tablespoons iced water. Continue blending until a nice smooth consistency. Season to taste with salt and freshly ground black pepper, and drizzle with extra virgin olive oil.

CURRY PASTES

Nowadays you can buy very good-quality pre-made curry pastes that are free from any MSG or other additives. Using store-bought curry paste makes cooking a curry a breeze and they last well in the fridge too. The strength (concentration) and hotness (chilli content) can differ significantly between brands, so choose according to your preference. The authentic curry pastes we use in our recipes are quite concentrated so if the brand you use is not as strongly flavoured, you may have to add more than the recipe states. If your curry needs more flavour, you can always add more curry paste to it. However, it is important that you first cook the curry paste out separately with a few tablespoons of coconut cream, before adding it to the curry. Simply adding raw uncooked curry paste straight into the curry sauce will not bring out its flavours.

Thai Red Curry Paste
Makes 1 cup

Soak 3–4 large whole dried chillies in boiling hot water for 15 minutes until soft, then drain. Place in a food processor along with 5 shallots, peeled and chopped, 1 tablespoon ground coriander, 1½ tablespoons grated fresh ginger, 4 cloves garlic, chopped, 2 stalks lemongrass, tough outer layer removed and remainder finely chopped, 3 kaffir lime leaves, tough central stem removed and leaves finely chopped, 1½ teaspoons salt, 1 teaspoon dried shrimp paste, 2 tablespoons tomato paste, 1 teaspoon ground turmeric and 2 tablespoons olive oil. Blend until smooth. Heat 1 tablespoon oil in a medium fry-pan on medium heat and cook curry paste for a few minutes until very fragrant and thickened.

Thai Green Curry Paste
Makes 1 cup

Follow recipe for Thai red curry paste above, but use 4–5 whole green chillies in place of the dried red chillies, and add 1 teaspoon crushed black peppercorns.

Panang Curry Paste
Panang curry paste is very similar to red curry paste, but is milder and sweeter with less chilli and the addition of peanuts. Follow recipe above for red curry paste, but use only 1–2 large whole dried chillies (Panang curry is a lot more mild), and add ¼–⅓ cup finely crushed peanuts (or crunchy peanut butter).

Tandoori Paste
Makes ½ cup

Mix together 1 tablespoon ground cumin, 2 teaspoons ground coriander, 1 tablespoon smoked paprika, 1 teaspoon ground turmeric, ½–1 teaspoon ground chilli, 1 teaspoon minced fresh ginger, 2 cloves garlic, finely minced, 2 tablespoons tomato paste, 1 teaspoon salt and 2 tablespoons natural unsweetened yoghurt.

SALAD DRESSINGS
A good dressing can make all the difference to a salad. Here are some of our favourites that will jazz up any of your salads. Unless specified, these dressings will keep in the fridge for weeks.

Lime and Fish Sauce Dressing
Great for any Asian-style salad, but also leafy green salads.

Makes ½ cup

Combine 1 tablespoon fish or soy sauce, ¼ cup lime juice, 2 teaspoons brown sugar, 2 teaspoons sesame oil and 1 tablespoon vegetable oil (e.g. peanut, canola, rice bran or soy).

Ponzu Dressing
Ponzu is a delicious and refreshing Japanese dressing that combines soy sauce and citrus.

Makes 1 cup

Combine ⅓ cup lime or lemon juice, ⅓ cup soy sauce, 1 tablespoon rice vinegar, 2 teaspoons sesame oil, 2 teaspoons sugar or mirin and 1 tablespoon vegetable oil (e.g. canola, rice bran or soy).

Red Wine Vinegar Dressing
A classic dressing great for any type of salad.

Makes ½ cup

Combine 3 tablespoons red wine vinegar, juice of ½ lemon, 3 tablespoons extra virgin olive oil, 2 teaspoons runny honey and 1 teaspoon wholegrain mustard.

Creamy Dressing
We use this dressing for coleslaws and potato salads. It is much lighter than using plain mayonnaise, and much nicer too we find!

Makes ½ cup

Combine ¼ cup mayonnaise, ¼ cup natural thick Greek yoghurt, 2 teaspoons Dijon mustard and juice of ½ lemon. Will keep in fridge for a few days.

Soy and Hoisin Dressing
This is an incredibly useful dressing for any Asian-style noodle dish or salad. The hoisin adds a characteristic sweet and subtle spiciness.

Makes ½ cup

Combine 3 tablespoons hoisin sauce, 1½ tablespoons sesame oil, 1½ tablespoons soy sauce and 1½ tablespoons rice vinegar.

Basic Sweet Chilli Dressing
Makes ½ cup

Combine 2 tablespoons sweet chilli sauce, 3 tablespoons lemon or lime juice and 2 tablespoons extra virgin olive oil. Will keep in fridge for a week.

Asian Sweet Chilli Dressing
Makes ½ cup

Add 2 teaspoons fish sauce and 1 teaspoon sesame oil to the basic sweet chilli dressing (above). Will keep in fridge for a week.

Honey Mustard Dressing
This is another classic dressing, like the red wine vinegar dressing, great for any type of salad.

Makes ½ cup

Combine 3 tablespoons red or white wine vinegar, 1½ tablespoons runny honey, 3 tablespoons extra virgin olive oil and 1 teaspoon wholegrain mustard.

Herb Vinaigrette
Makes ½ cup

Combine 1 tablespoon finely chopped thyme leaves, 3–4 tablespoons finely chopped basil leaves, 3 tablespoons extra virgin olive oil, 3 tablespoons lemon juice and season to taste with salt and pepper.

OTHER

Homemade Pizza Bases
Makes 4 bases

1 cup lukewarm water
1 tablespoon active dried yeast
1 teaspoon sugar
450g high-grade flour
1 tablespoon olive oil
1 teaspoon salt

1. Put water in a bowl and add yeast and sugar. Stir gently and leave in a warm place until yeast has dissolved and mixture is very frothy. Mix well.

2. Place flour, olive oil and salt in a large mixing bowl. Add yeast mixture and mix well to form a dough. (Note: there may be some leftover flour in the bowl once you've formed the dough, this is fine.)

3. Knead dough for 8–10 minutes until smooth and elastic (when you push in a finger the dough should bounce back), then place in an oiled bowl. Cover with a tea towel or cling film and leave in a warm place to rise until double in size (about 40 minutes).

4. Once dough has risen, knock it back by punching it with your fist (to knock out some of the air), then cut into 4 pieces. Roll out each pizza base on a floured surface into a roughly shaped disc, about 20cm in diameter (they should be nice and thin to help them go nice and crispy). Your pizza bases are now ready to use!

Caramelised Onions
Caramelised onions make a great burger filling and pizza topping. Make a big batch and keep in an airtight container in the fridge for a few days.

Heat a drizzle of olive oil in a medium fry-pan on medium heat. Cook 1 onion, thinly sliced, for about 10 minutes or until starting to caramelise. If at any time the onion is starting to catch on the bottom of the pan and burn, just add a splash of water. Add 2 teaspoons brown sugar and 1½ tablespoons balsamic vinegar and continue to cook for a further 2–3 minutes or until dark and slightly sticky.

A Note on Chipotle Sauce
This is a spicy sauce made from chipotle chillies (smoked dried jalapeno chillies). You can find this with specialty sauces at any supermarket. It is a great accompaniment to Mexican cooking, giving heat and a characteristic smoky flavour.

A Note on White Miso Paste
Miso, a staple in Japanese cooking, is made by fermenting soybeans with other ingredients. The result is a thick paste which is used for sauces, spreads, pickling, and mixed with dashi (soup stock) to make into the commonly known miso soup. It adds a salty and savoury (umami) flavour to dishes. You will be able to find it in the Japanese section of any supermarket, often in large tubs that will last in the fridge for weeks.

Bottom image opposite
The test kitchen chefs. From left:
Anton (Allspice) Leyland, Polly (Pomegranate)
Brodie, Mike (Gremolata) Grieg, Nadia
(Lemongrass) Lim, Kay (Guacamole) Glendining,
Nikki (Juniper) Jost, Dani (Daikon) Pearson.

INDEX

ACKNOWLEDGEMENTS

Writing this book has been a wonderful experience — made easy with such a bright, fun and enthusiastic team of foodies in the My Food Bag test kitchens in both Sydney and Auckland. We love working with you; you're an incredible, dedicated dream team — thanks so much!

A very special mention needs to be made of Polly (Pomegranate) Brodie for working so hard on this book — you've been a rock star! Likewise, every member of our test kitchen should take a bow: thanks for the laughter, delicious food, styling know-how and every-day brilliance. Anton (Allspice) Leyland for leading this charge, Mike (Gremolata) Greig, Kay (Guacamole) Glendining, Dani (Daikon) Pearce, Nicola (Juniper) Jost, Hannah (Harissa) Gilbert, Kylie (Dijon) Day, Lana (Lemon) Eade and Ginny (Ginger) Grant — you are a delight to work with.

A book needs to look delicious too, so a very special thank you to photographer Tam West and stylist Victoria Bell — who we've aptly named Tam Tamarillo and Victoria Blueberry — for making us want to eat the pages!

Likewise a big high-five to the Auckland-based team at Strategy Design and Advertising for pulling the design together and producing yet another stunning cookbook. Big thanks to Jenny Hellen and the entire team at Allen & Unwin (on both sides of the Tasman): you're a fantastic, hard-working team and we love your work! Also Rebecca Lal and Sarah Ell, thank you so much for your editing, proofing and ongoing guidance.

The teams of clever young marketers — Harriet (Hummus) Munro, Becks (Butternut) Bradley, Matt (Pepper) Paul, and Rory (Radish) Turley — thanks for all of your input. Likewise to our senior leadership team both in Australia and New Zealand, Suzanne (Mentsuyu) Mitchell, Fiona (Fennel) McCauley, Anton (Allspice) Leyland, Richard (Wagyu) Wafer, Keiran (Korma) Andersen, Luke (Linguine) Smith and Catherine (Capsicum) George for all of your dedication and drive.

Finally our customers (from Apple to Zucchini!) — we love delivering you the goodness. You're an incredible group of people and we feel honoured to be part of your lives. Thanks so very much for your support, your messages and your love. This book is for you guys!

Nadia x

First published in 2016

Text and recipes copyright © My Food Bag 2016
Photography copyright © Tamara West 2016

Allen & Unwin
Level 3, 228 Queen Street
Auckland 1010, New Zealand
Phone: (64 9) 377 3800

83 Alexander Street
Crows Nest NSW 2065, Australia
Phone: (61 2) 8425 0100

Email: info@allenandunwin.com
Web: www.allenandunwin.co.nz

A catalogue record for this book is available from the National Library of New Zealand

ISBN 978 1 87750 565 2

Styling: Victoria Bell
Design: Strategy Design & Advertising

Printed by Hang Tai Printing Company Limited, China

10 9 8 7 6 5 4 3 2 1